NIGHT STALKER

The true story of Delroy Grant, Britain's
most shocking serial sex attacker

JOHN McSHANE

JOHN BLAKE

Published by John Blake Publishing Ltd,
3 Bramber Court, 2 Bramber Road,
London W14 9PB, England

www.johnblakepublishing.co.uk

www.facebook.com/Johnblakepub facebook
twitter.com/johnblakepub twitter

First published in paperback in 2011

ISBN: 978 1 84454 973 3

British Library Cataloguing-in-Publication Data:

A catalogue record for this book is available from the
British Library.

Design by www.envydesign.co.uk

Printed in Great Britain by CPI Bookmarque Ltd, Croydon CR0 4TD

1 3 5 7 9 10 8 6 4 2

Papers used by John Blake Publishing are natural, recyclable products
made from wood grown in sustainable forests. The manufacturing processes
conform to the environmental regulations of the country of origin.

CHAPTER ONE

It was October, so by quarter-past nine that Sunday evening in 1992 it had already been dark for several hours. The old lady decided it was time for bed. She prepared herself in the way that women of her generation did: grooming and washing, brushing and cleaning. Half an hour later, she was in her cream and grey floral pyjamas and under the bedclothes. She had not said 'good night' to anyone: there was no one to say 'good night' to. The old woman had never married and ten years earlier had moved in with her then recently widowed sister; it seemed the natural thing to do. But her sister had died a few months earlier and since then the old woman had lived alone – her other sister was also dead – in the bungalow that was her home. It was her haven, her refuge. A safe place to spend the remaining years of her life.

1

The bay-windowed bedroom she slept in, with its grey curtains, dark-blue carpet and pink-patterned wallpaper, was at the front of her house. Her home, with its typical white lift-up garage double-doors, overlooked a neat lawn and carefully trimmed garden which sloped gently towards a hip-high brick wall. On the other side of the wall was a broad pavement and a busy road that would be packed in a few hours with suburban traffic as it was every Monday morning: men and women hurrying to work or on their way to dropping off children at school, lorry drivers already behind schedule, angry men at the wheels of white vans hoping to cross the nearby intersection before the lights changed. Beyond those traffic lights lay a small collection of shops; a chemist, newsagents, grocers and Indian and Chinese take-ways. They were in that hinterland in Shirley, Croydon, where south London, Kent and Surrey merge into one. It was suburbia personified, the kind of place where nothing much ever seemed to happen.

The woman's room was small, about 11ft by 11ft, with the bed in the middle and a chair on one side of it. In the room was a 2ft-high black safe, opened by a key, not a combination. Her bedside lamp gave off just enough light to enable her ageing eyes to see at night. Reading for a short while was usually all it took to help her get to sleep – a few pages and she would drift off. That's what happened most nights, but this was not to be an ordinary evening. She heard a sound of some sort, a knocking she thought, but was unable to discern exactly what it was.

Living by a bustling road, she thought no more of it. Perhaps, as it transpired, it was a terrible mistake to make. Because she could not settle, she decided a drink was needed, and went into the kitchen to make a cup of coffee. Afterwards, a look at the kitchen clock told her that it was now 10.30pm, so she returned to bed and decided to read for a few minutes more. It was late for her, it was time to sleep. She was, after all, 89 years old.

In 1903, when she was born, Queen Victoria had only been dead two years and the sun still never set on the British Empire. A young man by the name of Winston Churchill had recently become an MP, Wilbur and Orville Wright had yet to take to the air for the first manned flight, and the *Titanic* had not even been built, let alone sunk in its icy grave. It was all so long ago and so many things had happened in the years since she was born: two world wars, the invention of television and the discovery of penicillin were still decades away. What times she had lived through. She deserved a good night's sleep, a rest. At that age, it was the least that she was entitled to.

What she didn't know – and how could she? – was that someone was watching that anonymous bungalow where she lived. He was watching that night as he had watched many nights before. Those cold, merciless, calculating eyes were taking everything in. Days too: he was relentless in his observations. The homes he was to target had to be occupied by the elderly and they had to live alone.

He looked for handrails near the front door, ramps for

easier access, solitary milk bottles on doorsteps, the elderly moving gently inside and possibly slowly outside the building or nervously answering callers through a front door opened just a few inches to protect against possible intruders. He didn't want to make any mistakes so he noted everything as he waited for his moment, the right time to strike.

He wanted to be sure of his ground, that the victim had no means of resisting him, that no one else would be in the house. No other occupant, no other visitor. No young, healthy, strong, relative paying an unscheduled overnight visit who might emerge from a spare bedroom and challenge him in the darkness he would create in the 16ft-long hall that ran through the heart of the bungalow. There had to be only one person there. They had to be old and frail. They had to be defenceless. They had to be at his mercy. That would make everything he intended to do so much easier. Perhaps too it made it all that more thrilling, knowing that he was the one with the power and they were incapable of self-defence.

The 89-year-old lady in that bungalow was exactly the type of victim he had in mind. She fitted the bill to perfection. Whatever he did to her, however heartless and cruel he was to be, she had no escape. No danger of any resistance or retaliation for him to overcome, no one to hear her cries of help, her pleas for leniency or restraint. The aged voice appealing for decency would go unheard.

Everything would be in darkness. The terrifying blackness of the night would be relieved only by the light from the torch in his gloved hand. He would be in control of that too: he had the power of light and dark, night and day, all at the touch of one of his fingers. That was how he liked it. There would be no phone to reach for and, with trembling, wrinkled fingers, dial for help, even if she were capable of doing so. The telephone line had been cut. The only person who could free her would be her attacker himself, a strong young man in his thirties, and that release would only come if and when he showed her compassion. And he was not in the mood to show clemency. That wasn't what he did that night nor in nearly two decades of brutality and perversion that followed. His victims were always defenceless. Always old, always someone he had power over. Elderly women and men whose physical frailty and mental confusion meant that he had the upper hand in the darkness. He would be in control. He always had to be in control.

Back in bed, the old woman tried to sleep, unaware of the terror which was so soon to come into her life and was to stay with her for the rest of her days. After a few minutes, the door to the small bedroom slowly opened and there was the figure of a man in the doorway. The nightmare was to begin for her as it was for so many more in the years to come.

The man in the doorway moved swiftly to her bedside and told her to be quiet. He was wearing a grey pullover, a dark jacket and dark trousers. Over his head was a balaclava which meant that the only part of him that could be seen were his eyes.

'What are you doing here?' she asked. It was a question that many more were to ask him. Some used those same words; others might vary the phrase slightly. Some merely thought it to themselves. Deep in their hearts, however, even as they uttered the words, they knew the answer. Or at least they thought they did.

Placing a gloved hand over her mouth he told her, 'Be quiet.'

Eventually, the terrified woman was able to ask him, 'What do you want? Money?'

He said nothing, but she opened her purse and gave him all the money that she had in it, two £10 notes and one £5 note. He wasn't satisfied; he wasn't the type to be so easily dismissed. With one hand he took the money, and with the other he grabbed her handbag. 'They told me you had a lot of money.'

All she could reply was: 'No, that's all I've got.' She'd still had enough wits about her to take the safe keys out of her handbag and put them underneath the mattress as she sat up in the bed.

The stranger walked around the room, checking letters and papers. He was restless and moved the curtain slightly to one side, no doubt to ensure that there was no one outside who might hear any cries of distress. Then he returned to the bedside where he took out the light bulb near the bed and then the main one from the ceiling, before walking into the hall where he did the same.

He pushed her back on the bed and took hold of the waistband of her pyjamas. She cried out to him, 'Stop! Stop!

Leave me alone!' All the time, she was trying to push him away, but it was useless. She was too old and frail; he was too young and powerful. He managed to get her trousers down to hip-level only for her to bravely pull them up again.

He now put his hands on either side of the old woman's head to hold it still and began to kiss her face, pressing his lips against hers and trying to force his tongue into her mouth. Again she told him, 'Stop it please! You are hurting me!'

There was no reply. Her pleas went unheeded: he did not care. The stranger pulled her pyjamas down again and raped her, his hands pressing so fiercely and with such power against her old face that her false teeth came out of her mouth.

His eyes then alighted on the safe and, despite her protests that it was not hers and she had no keys, he soon discovered them. After opening it with the key, he pulled out a drawer and took out a brown wallet containing £250 and some jewellery: a gold chain, two rings, an old coin and a hunter pocket watch, the kind only seen nowadays in TV costume dramas.

The old woman, attacked and abused, feared that there was worse to come. 'I was worried what he was going to do next. I have seen on television what people have done to old people. I was worried he was going to slash me,' she said later.

Instead, he went to the front door and bolted it at the top and bottom. Then, still seeing only by the light of the torch in his hand, he went towards the kitchen – the room, it was later discovered, through which he had gained entry. Leaving by the back door, he disappeared into the darkness from which he had emerged two terrifying hours earlier.

Aged as she was, the old lady moved some steps so that she could replace one of the ceiling light bulbs and then tried to phone for help. What followed was a scene that would be replayed many times over the next 17 years: the discovery that the telephone line had been cut, followed by a panic-stricken attempt to contact a relative or neighbour who, on hearing details of the break-in and what had followed, would show first disbelief and then incomprehension at the enormity and vileness of what had taken place.

As quickly as she could, the old lady put some clothes on over her nightwear and, with her stockings around her knees, went to her niece's home nearby. There she pressed the bell and, when the woman's husband answered the door, she told him she had been burgled. While he went into the kitchen to telephone the police, the woman took her agitated aunt into the living room. When she asked why she hadn't telephoned, the old lady said her line had been cut. Then came the astonishing revelation: 'He raped me.'

The niece was so amazed she could not believe her ears. 'Are you sure?' she asked and back came the answer 'Yes.' The dishevelled old lady, the scratches on her face now visible, was pacing around the room, and even though her niece urged her to sit down she could not.

Alas, there was little she could do to help the police with a description of her balaclava-wearing attacker. 'I would not recognise him if I saw him again. I did not know if he had an accent because he did not say much,' she said. She described him as about 6ft tall and 22 years old. He was black with brown eyes, but that was about it.

This was, of course, exactly as her attacker had planned it. How could an old, confused and violated woman be able to give an accurate, detailed description at the best of times? In this case, with the man's distinguishing features all but hidden, it was impossible.

There was more heartache and distress in store for the victim that seemingly endless night. When the police arrived, there were procedures that had to be followed and, no matter how tactfully or compassionately these matters were approached, they were bound to upset the old lady. The victim was taken to a special suite for victims of sexual assaults, where she was examined by a male doctor and swabs were taken.

A woman detective constable, specially trained in 'chaperoning' rape victims, was among the police who arrived. The detective, experienced in cases similar to this one, was later to recall, 'I saw a small, frail elderly woman … She was clearly upset and was shaking slightly. I remained with her and she held my hand tightly and she was crying throughout. She was looking at the wall and the examination lasted 10 to 15 minutes. The victim then said, "I wish I had never reported it now." I had tears in my eyes as she said that to me.'

Even as that heart-rending examination was taking place, police were scouring the scene of the crime at the victim's bungalow. A detective constable from South Norwood had been told there'd been an aggravated burglary at the home and, in the bedroom that had been the scene of the elderly woman's terror, he found a pair of pyjama bottoms in a heap on the floor with slippers and socks. All were placed in bags and sent to the Metropolitan Police Forensic Science Laboratory.

The pyjama bottoms were semen-stained and that, as we will see later, was to provide one of the clues in the hunt for the woman's attacker.

And what of the old lady, crying with shame and torment on an examination couch? Again, we will look at the effects on her, and her family, more closely later on. Suffice to say that she moved in with her relatives after that night. Daytimes she seemed all right, but in the evening she became nervous and did not want to be alone. Once, the family looking after her were late returning home and she remonstrated with them saying, 'I thought you were never coming back.' The next day, full of remorse, she bought them a gift as a way of saying sorry: a bottle of sherry.

She declined counselling – that wasn't for her. Instead, she would go back to the bungalow in the daytime without telling anyone, only giving away her secret by returning before dark fell with belongings she could only have retrieved from there. After a couple of months, she moved to a first-floor flat, which she immediately examined to see how secure it was. She saw that there was a sloping porch roof directly below her large window, so she never opened that window. She also worried constantly about a loft hatch in the ceiling.

Her long life, in which she had seen no fewer than 19 Prime Ministers in power, eventually came to an end when she died in 2005, over 100 years after she was born.

The terrible legacy from the evening of her attack until her death 13 years later was that she never again spent a night in the bungalow that had been her home for so long. That terrifying moment when the man who was to become known as the Night Stalker came into her life left such a lasting impact on her that she could not face the prospect.

And what caring, civilised person could blame her?

CHAPTER TWO

It is a building that has conquered the world, yet few homes have been the subject of as much disdain as the bungalow. They are sneered at, pitied and lampooned, their occupants treated with a mixture of indifference and mockery.

The word is derived from the Indian *bengalo*, used to describe homes popular in the Bengal region: small, low structures invariably with a veranda. 'Bungalow' has been used in the English language for over 400 years, initially for hovels where sailors could spend the night when ashore in India, but subsequently for much more prestigious houses. The passion for these functional low-rise homes soon spread: Australia, Canada, Ireland, California and the US all developed distinctive bungalow styles that are still popular to this day.

The bungalow boom in Britain came between the two

world wars, with vast numbers being built in areas on the nicer outskirts of cities or in coastal towns within sight of the sea. Sneered at by the chattering classes but adored by many of the masses, especially the retired or physically impaired, for their ease of maintenance and lack of tiring, difficult stairs to cope with, bungalows became an integral part of the nation's backdrop. Bungalow-land became, albeit unfairly, synonymous with a Little Britain mentality of respectability, privacy, neatness and functionality.

Rock stars, avant-garde artists, revolutionaries did not live in bungalows. Nice, ordinary, ageing, decent people did. They liked bungalows for all the right reasons. Delroy Grant liked them too, for all the wrong ones.

Grant knew you didn't need a ladder to get into a bungalow and invariably there would be gardens and hedges to hide in while he watched the buildings and their inhabitants. The neighbouring homes would probably be of the same, low height, so there was no chance of being spotted by a neighbour looking down from a higher window and catching sight of Grant as he carried out his reconnaissance. On and on stretched 'boring' suburbia with its abundance of bungalows and homes for the elderly; the cul-de-sacs, the crescents, the tree-lined avenues were all perfect for him too.

The hunting ground enjoyed by Grant was a long way from his own roots, geographically and socially. Delroy Easton Grant had a midwife-assisted birth at his parents' modest home in Spanish Town Road, Kingston, Jamaica on 3 September 1957. His father George earned a living, as he puts it, 'buying and selling' – in other words, as a market trader from a stall in the island's capital. His mother Vida was a domestic worker.

George and Vida were not a couple for long, however. One day, George saw her at a bus stop with another man and the inevitable confrontation ensued, followed shortly by Vida's admission that she was in a relationship with this man. George and Vida split acrimoniously and he moved her belongings out of the home they shared together. She later left for a new life in America, and Grant was later to say that he 'did not know' his mother: she made no attempt to contact him nor he her.

George had never married Vida and eventually formed a relationship with his wife-to-be, Ruby. Like many of his generation, he departed for Britain around this time, leaving behind not only Delroy but also two other sons, Trevor and Michael. Trevor was the oldest and Michael was the youngest of the trio, all of whom had different mothers. So, from about the age of four, little Delroy was brought up by George's mother, Blanche Grant, in the largely agricultural area of St Catherine, some 30 miles from the capital Kingston.

In England, George, who was eventually to work for British Rail for 19 years putting up posters on billboards and hoardings, lived in rented accommodation in south London for a number of years before he and Ruby bought their small terraced home in East Dulwich in the early 1970s. George sent money back to Jamaica to help with the boy's upkeep and he also visited four or five times in that ten-year period, when he could afford the fare, and made a point of seeing Delroy. Whenever it came time to say goodbye to his son, little Delroy would always cry.

Eventually, there came a time when Delroy became too troublesome for his grandmother to cope with – not in itself an unusual thing to happen – and he had to leave the island of his birth and head to London, as many teenagers before him had done and many more were to do. Reunited with his father, he went to Kingsdale School in West Dulwich, which, when it opened in 1958, had been hailed as one of London's new utopian comprehensives where children of all abilities would learn and where 'nobody would be allowed to feel a failure'.

However, in the years that followed, the school – very near the prestigious fee-paying Dulwich College – became known as a recruiting ground for local gangs: the Brixton Boys, the Dulwich Crew and in recent years the YPB (Young Peckham Boys). One report of the school said, 'Middle-class parents fled from the school en masse. Girls simply stopped coming.' Grant was later to say that he got on 'fairly well' at school but he left 'at the normal age' with no qualifications.

It was not to be an easy transition from the sunshine of the Caribbean to the streets of London. He was in his early teens and he would not even talk to his stepmother, Ruby, unless he had to. Grant put it this way: 'Life was all right, but I found my parents quite restrictive. They were good parents but fairly strict. That's the way we were brought up in Jamaica.'

The Grants may have been living in busy south London, but their home life was still based on Jamaican roots. His father and stepmother were devout churchgoers, Baptists, and believed in old-fashioned values. A painting of Christ is among the religious artefacts that adorn George Grant's home to this day. His father would tell the truculent teenager that he had to be home by 10pm or 10.30pm, but he would be ignored: his son would come home late or, at times, not at all.

Grant showed an interest in cricket while at school – it was the era of the great West Indian side led by Clive Lloyd and its dashing young batsman Viv Richards destroying bowling attacks around the world – and he played for a pub team in later years. He loved Bob Marley and wanted to play music so loud on the family's gramophone in the bay window of the living room that his father bought him his own record player to use in his bedroom.

After he left school, he got a job working as a mechanic and on the forecourt at a garage. On one occasion, when he stormed out of the parental home saying he was leaving and not coming back, his father had to go round to the garage and persuade his son's boss to continue employing him.

Grant now began a series of criminal offences that would continue into the 1990s. None of them, however, was similar to the crimes that were to bring him notoriety. He began in 1975 and 1976 at Tower Bridge Magistrates' Court, where he appeared for taking away a car and false accounting. He soon graduated to more serious charges and in August 1980 he was sentenced to two years in prison for his part in a robbery and for possessing an imitation firearm.

The first his father knew of the firearms charge was from a neighbour. 'I couldn't believe it when I heard,' he said. 'I just could not believe it.'

'I started mixing with some guys in a pub,' was his son's explanation of how that happened. They had played pool together and he eventually became the getaway driver for his pals in a raid on a post office. 'I went along with them and they got away with nothing,' he said later.

After his release, it was not long before he was in the dock again, this time in 1982 for obtaining property by deception. He received a suspended sentence, and a second suspended sentence followed in 1985 for using a false instrument. Convictions for criminal damage and possessing an offensive weapon followed, and in 1990 he was in court again for handling stolen goods. His long list – there were ten convictions in all – ended in September 1999 when he served a short sentence for handling stolen goods. None of his offences was of a sexual nature.

From his late teens until his final arrest, Grant had a string of women lovers. Some he married, some he did not. Some he introduced to his family first, some he did not. He also fathered at least eight children by four of these women, as well as becoming a stepfather to two more youngsters. His complex, sometimes violent, relationships with the women in his life – often seeing at least two at the same time – are something that we will return to later and see what affect, if any, they had on his behaviour.

In between these court appearances, Grant appeared to be a regular sort of guy. He liked his sport, drank Guinness at the local British Legion in south east London where he lived with his second wife, and had a variety of jobs: decorator, delivering for builders' merchants, mini-cab driving and operating his sound system Sir Cosmic Sound.

With sickening irony, he even carried out community service in an old people's home just one year before his first recorded attack. It was a result of the first sentence for handling stolen goods. He was given a 200-hour community service order after admitting handling a stolen cash card and cheques from a burglary. As he had moved to Leicestershire to be close to the woman he was in a relationship with at the time, he was ordered to carry out his sentence there. He was given a choice of locations, but chose to help out at a residential care home. It was 1991, and the next year the Night Stalker struck for the first time, raping his 89-year-old victim.

Perhaps that spell, albeit a brief one, of working with the elderly played a key role in Grant's subsequent perversion. In many of his attacks, he would lead his victims from one part of the house to another, holding on to them to give them support. Perhaps it was a skill he learned back in the early 1990s, or perhaps it was the proximity to their vulnerability then that first aroused his morbid interest in the elderly. Only Grant himself can answer that question, assuming he actually knows the answer.

And he is the only one who can say how often he struck either as a burglar or as a man carrying out sexual acts on the helpless. For the exact total of attacks will never be known, as many of his victims were either too confused to know what had happened or too ashamed to tell anyone about the mysterious caller in the night, even though they were innocent victims. It was not something they would have wanted to discuss and no doubt many have taken their secret to the grave.

It seems virtually inconceivable that, after that (presumably) initial attack in 1992, the Night Stalker remained inactive for most of the 1990s. What is certain, however, is that, by the night of 4 September 1998, he was ready to strike again.

CHAPTER THREE

Six years after the horror attack on the 89-year-old lady in Shirley, the Night Stalker struck again. This time, his victim was 81 years old. She suffered from chronic arthritis and needed her wooden walking stick to help her move, as she had both her hips replaced some years earlier. The nature of her condition was such that she had difficulty in rising from a chair or sitting up in bed. She was on several types of medication, including some for high blood pressure, and when winter arrived it always caused her a certain amount of wheeziness. She and her husband had moved into their bungalow in Warlingham in Surrey some 11 years earlier, but he had been dead for some time now so she lived alone.

The bungalow was in a residential cul-de-sac. It had a small front garden and a larger one to the rear, which had a modest summer house in it. There were patio doors from the lounge to the back garden, and to the rear were some new houses that had been built about five years earlier. The main door into the home was at the side of the bungalow and there was a wooden gate with a small fence on either side. The gate was always open so that dustmen and other callers could gain access. It was also useful for the paperboy who dropped in a newspaper around 7am daily and the milkman who left a pint of milk every day except Wednesday and Thursday. It was perfect for Delroy Grant too.

The elderly widow usually kept the kitchen door locked and there were locks on the internal doors too. Because of her mobility problems, she had a home help, and she was also visited by a friend who would shop for her. To give these people easier access to the house, there was a key to the back door kept outside, concealed from view, on a hook on the fence in the alleyway. During the course of his reconnaissance, Grant had either seen it used or discovered it himself and that was how he gained access to the woman's home. Easy pickings by his standard.

That night – Friday, 4 September 1998 – the old lady checked all the doors and made sure her front door was locked. She then went into the bathroom and had 'a quick swill' before slowly and painfully getting into bed around 11.30pm. She wore a pale-blue short-sleeve nightie and a pair of white knickers. Around her neck was a panic alarm that she placed over the bed.

Normally, she slept well, although her condition meant she had to sleep on her back. Once she had taken her various medication, she drifted off under the sheet and two blankets on her bed. In the middle of the night, perhaps about 2am, she awoke to find a man standing over her, roughly taking hold of her by the shoulders. 'Where's your money?' he said. 'I want your money.' She was later to remark, 'He spoke quite nicely. By that I mean he was well spoken.'

The old lady tried to speak but he put his hand over her mouth and threatened her. 'Shut up. Don't make a noise. Don't tell anyone.'

Bravely, she told him what she thought of him. 'I think you are thoroughly mean,' she said. 'I am 81, you know, and the shock could do anything.'

The intruder didn't care, though, and responded by holding her face even more tightly. He held it like that for about one minute, 60 seconds of fear and pain. Then the hooded figure began searching through her drawers, using his torch for light.

As was so often to be the case, the ordeal that his victim was experiencing soon moved on to a higher plain, one of sheer terror. After ten minutes, he turned his attention to her. He walked over to the bed and pulled down the sheet and blankets, lighting her nightclothes and removing her underwear. 'I thought the worst was going to happen,' she said later. 'By that I thought he was going to rape me.'

First, he indecently assaulted her and then pulled her aged, aching legs apart. 'It was incredibly painful due to my chronic arthritis.' she told police later. 'My feet would only go two feet apart.' Years later, this attack was described as 'a frightening and degrading experience' as well as being incredibly painful. 'I did not cry out but I got an attack of the wheezes,' the victim said. In an attempt to make her attacker stop, she pulled what she termed 'a horrid face', explaining, 'I hoped he would think I was seriously ill and stop doing what he was doing.'

After he had unsuccessfully tried to rape her, the attacker pulled the sheets and blankets back over her and then, in another bizarre act, felt her wrists as if he was trying to find a pulse. The attack had lasted about 15 minutes. He carried on with his search of her home but then left, empty-handed.

Her ordeal over, the elderly widow dozed off and when she awoke it was getting light. She needed to use the bathroom but, fearing that he might still be in the house, she waited for 15 minutes. Then slowly she moved around the house, using her stick to close the door through which he had exited and had left open. 'The bungalow was as tidy after the incident as it had been before,' she was to say. Afterwards, exhausted by her ordeal, she went back to sleep and awoke at 9am.

Victims of sex attacks, in shock and suffering from trauma, often do not behave in a rational way. Most people might expect the old lady to summon help immediately, but she did not do so, explaining in an almost logical, and certainly understandable, way: 'I did not tell anyone what had happened at this point because it had [ended] and all was well.'

But early that Saturday evening it began to get dark

and the fear returned, so at 7pm she telephoned her son. His wife answered the phone. 'I have got some bad news,' she told her daughter-in-law, who passed the phone over to her husband.

'Hi, Mum, what's the problem?' he said.

She told him that someone had been in the house and he, understandably, asked why it had taken her so long to tell him. 'I'm only ringing now because it is getting dark.'

Her son went to her home and when he arrived his mother was, by this time, watching television. She told him about the intruder but the full details of the attack only emerged later when police were called. 'I felt disappointed that my mum did not tell me from the outset. But I can understand. She was a private person; she was not the kind to volunteer information.'

When the police arrived at her bungalow at 10.40pm, the victim was wearing the same nightie she'd had on the previous evening; by now she was wrapped in a burgundy dressing gown as well. The police asked her to change, and her clothes and undergarments were taken away to Caterham police station for examination and forensic tests.

As with all the Night Stalker's victims, the description was vague: medium height, about 5 feet 5 inches tall, mid-twenties to mid-thirties, slender. 'I never saw his face. I just saw two eyes and they were possibly brown in colour. I did not see any skin. I do not know what colour skin he had.'

The female doctor who examined her found her 'a very

bright and intelligent lady' and discovered bruises to her jaw, forearm, elbow and wrist, injuries all caused by the attack. Swabs were also taken and the traces of the body fluids that were found were to play a crucial part in capturing the Night Stalker in years to come.

Back at the house, it was discovered that the key that had been kept outside was missing. A scene-of-crime officer also found that a small window to the victim's bedroom was slightly ajar and there was an indentation to the frame on the outside. Inside, on the same window frame, there were woollen glove marks. Police also took a swab of some of the man's body fluids from a stain on the bedroom carpet.

'It is a nasty feeling to know that a stranger has been through your home,' she said. 'During the incident, I feared the man was going to nobble me. By that I mean I was fearful he was going to finish me off. I was in no position to defend myself due to my age and infirmity. The assault was absolutely ghastly and I want to forget about it. However, I have to live with the fear that he will return.'

It had been almost six years between this attack and the case in Shirley in October 1992. Even that one may have been preceded by other, unrecorded offences. What is certain is that worse was to come: these two were not to be isolated cases. Although there had been a lull of several years, the Night Stalker became active again towards the end of the decade with a string of offences that bore the hallmark of crimes being committed by the same man:

access often gained through a window, lights and telephone disconnected, a balaclava-wearing figure threatening an elderly victim, sexual acts or assault.

It was decided that the fiend carrying out these raids had to be caught and Operation Minstead was launched. As was the custom at the time, any major investigation was named after a country village. As the selection was an alphabetical one and the letter 'M' had been reached, Minstead – in the New Forest in Hampshire – was chosen. None of the team involved could have been under any illusion that their task was to be an easy one, but neither could they have thought they would be part of the largest manhunt in Scotland Yard's history or that it would be over a decade before they got their man.

But all that lay in the future when, in the summer of 1999, the Night Stalker suddenly began a frenzied spate of attacks. The first was on the night of Saturday, 19 June, continuing into the early hours of the Sunday morning, Midsummer's Eve. It took place in Beckenham in Kent, and the victim was a 71-year-old woman who had lived there for over 40 years. She went to bed at midnight that evening and read a book for 45 minutes or so before falling asleep. As she slept in her bedroom at the front of her terraced house, the Stalker was busy removing the entire pane of glass from the kitchen window at the rear.

The victim was woken by a heavy weight across her body – it was her attacker. He had his right hand over her mouth and nose. The figure was dressed in black and all she could make out were his eyes staring into hers. 'I was absolutely petrified. I began to struggle but the man was strong.'

He put a pillow over her mouth. 'I was having difficulty breathing and struggled to get air,' she said later. There was worse to come. He put another pillow on her face and applied more pressure. 'It was at this point that I thought I was going to die and as a result gave up struggling. I could feel the weight of the man on top of me.'

She made a conscious decision to stop moving in the hope that he would stop applying the pressure. The intruder then said, 'Diamonds and money.' She said she would get her purse but then saw he had already found it. He then began to go through her chest of drawers using the light from his torch. 'Where's your husband?' he asked her, and she said he was in London, working. The man asked what he did and she replied, 'Security.'

While the man was busy going through the drawers, the victim reached across her bed and hit her panic alarm. It sounded one quick blast, but he quickly ripped it away from her and angrily snapped it in two. He also threw the useless handset of the phone on the bed and she noticed that there was no sign of life coming from her electric clock; the power had been switched off in the house.

Then he said, 'I want oral sex with you.' The victim could not bear the thought of what he was telling her, and in her fear asked that she might be allowed to go to the bathroom to get a glass of water.

He gripped her tightly by the arm as, wearing just her

nightie, she walked along the corridor towards the bathroom. But she was not going to give up without a fight. 'I swung my right hand towards the man's groin with the intention of hitting him where it hurts.' She missed and the amber tumbler she had in her hand smashed against the wall. She did, however, succeed in knocking the torch out of his hand, and anxiously he began to look for it. His normal routine destroyed, he fled the house by the back door after a stay of about 20 minutes and the woman crossed the road to alert a neighbour.

She later discovered he had taken valuable diamond rings, a bracelet and approximately £100 in cash. Police were to find a scarf with saliva on it that years later would provide another DNA link to Grant.

One of the most disturbing aspects of the Night Stalker's reign of terror was not just the immediate effect his crimes had on the victims, but the lingering aftermath, the legacy he left them. A decade after he had attacked her and violated the home that she had lived in for 43 years, his victim in this case summed it up like this:

'Before I was burgled I was very outgoing. I used to go out and about dancing with friends all over London, mostly ballroom dancing and the odd tea dances. I'd also go out to the cinema, the theatre, lots of social dances, at all times of day or night. I drove back then, and my friends and I would take it in turns to drive. I would go dancing about five times a week. I also took part in voluntary work once a month with the local church. A group of us would go to London from 8pm to 1am to distribute clothes and provisions to the homeless in central London. I really enjoyed my life.

'Health-wise I was in good health, only the odd cough or cold here or there – touch wood – but otherwise I was fine. I was security conscious and very secure in my home. I always kept my curtains drawn at night and my windows were locked.

'On 20 June 1999, this man broke into my home. What terrified me was that he got through a window that was triple-locked while I was in bed in the middle of the night. It shattered my feeling of being secure in my home. Immediately after this incident and indeed up until now, I do not sleep well out of the fear that I will be attacked in my home. The fear keeps me awake.

'Every noise upsets me. I'm very nervous at sounds that I don't recognise. The day after this incident, I saw my GP and I was a blubbering wreck. I remember he made a note of all my bruising. I had bruises all down my arms.

'I can't remember if I had any other injuries – in fact, there is much I can't remember about the incident. I've buried it and have had to dig to remember. I really don't want to dig, I don't want to go there. The man made me feel very vulnerable. I didn't know what he was going to do to me.

'I stopped going out in the evenings after that. I would go to afternoon matinees but I always make sure I am home before dark. Even when I visit friends or relatives, I make sure they bring me home in good time. When they drop me at home, I always make sure they search every room in the house and check every lock on the doors and the windows. I'm quite obsessive about that being done, but my family, the children and even the grandchildren just do it naturally now – check the house, that is.

'After the burglary, I moved back in on my own. I felt I had to. For peace of mind my daughter and her husband took time off and installed a burglar alarm, not sure how much it cost. As I said before, I stopped dancing five times a week and only went to afternoon shows. My friends were very understanding.

'About 18 months after the incident, I had a stroke. I can't remember what caused it, but since then I've been on high blood pressure medication. I was paralysed in my right arm and lost the use of my voice. I had to have speech therapy because I was speaking gobbledegook. The use of my right arm came back. I've been very lucky really.

'The police installed a panic alarm in my house, I can't remember when. It was a good feeling to know that if I pressed that button the police would be there almost immediately. I felt more secure when I had that alarm. When I was told that the alarm had to be removed because of costs and the new radio not being all right for the alarm, it caused me a lot of distress and when eventually it was taken away I felt very insecure again.

'I am now very wary of people. I get claustrophobia when people stand too close to me and give slim black men a very wide berth when I'm on the streets or at the bus stop, because at the back of my mind I'm saying,

"Is it him?" My GP has been keeping an eye on me since the incident and I'm now on high blood pressure tablets for life.

'When I'm in, all my doors – that is, the porch and back doors – are always kept locked. I have to draw the curtains when it gets dark because I hate seeing the dark. This man has totally unsettled my life. I don't go out as I used to, he's ruined my life. I would like this man to be locked up away from everyone for a long time so that he can no longer be a menace to the rest of the community. Preferably for the rest of his life.

'I try not to think about this incident, I'm always pushing it back. It is the only way I can get on with my life.'

That long summer of 1999 saw an increase in the known activities of Delroy Grant. Perhaps he was getting an increased kick, possibly the long hours of daylight helped as he carried out reconnaissance or it could be that he was in greater need of money.

His next known target again fell into the perfect demographic of his victims: she was 77, a widow and she had lived alone for eight years. In this case, though, Grant was unable to get into her semi-detached bungalow. It was only because of an attack near her home that police called and asked her if she had seen anything suspicious. She pointed out marks around her metal patio doors. He had failed, for once, to gain entry, although the marks he left were later to form part of the case against him. Perhaps the task was too difficult or he might have been disturbed.

Either way, she had been one of the lucky ones. The same could not be said of Grant's next victim, an 83-year-old Parkinson's Disease sufferer – and a man.

CHAPTER FOUR

The Night Stalker's abuse of the elderly was not confined to women. Men were among his victims too. All were liable to attack: no one was safe.

The 83-year-old widower who was Delroy Grant's next target lived alone in a bungalow in Coulsdon, Surrey. It had a typical layout with a driveway at the front and a garden at the back. The Parkinson's Disease from which he suffered affected his memory and meant he needed a stick to walk with. It also meant his hearing and sight were affected. He had lived alone since his wife died seven years earlier, although he was visited by a home help and by his sons. Occasionally, there would be someone at the door asking if he needed any jobs doing, but he would say no as he'd had a bad experience when one of these callers tried to charge for work they hadn't done. Once bitten, twice shy.

The widower tried to go out for a daily walk when he could and would occasionally attend Blind Association dinners in Croydon. Most Thursdays, he would go to morning meetings at church, and on Friday mornings he would be taken to Waitrose to shop 'because it's less busy than Tesco'. He put it in the simple way that summed up his generation and the existence they led. 'Life follows a routine which has been the same for years,' he said, adding, 'Life is quiet.'

That routine and the tranquillity he enjoyed were to come to a savage end on the night of Saturday, 3 July 1999. He went to bed at 10pm and quickly fell asleep, but in the early hours he woke up suddenly to find a figure looming over him by the bed. The stranger, torch in hand, said something like, 'Give me the money' or 'Find me the money.' Whatever the exact words were, the message was clear. The uninvited guest smelled of 'stale sweat' but there was no trace of alcohol or smoke on his breath.

The old man said he only kept £5 in the bungalow for emergencies. 'It was clear he did not believe me as he repeated it two or three times. Without warning, he picked me up and frogmarched me into the lounge.' Once there, the man added, 'He started to punch me; he punched me hard several times before I could take it no more.'

The victim showed his attacker a wooden box in which he kept some cash, £17, and then he was frogmarched back into the bedroom. He forced his knee between the elderly man's legs and then indecently assaulted him. When the victim fought back, Grant struck him again. 'I had been frightened before, but this was much, much worse. As we struggled, he took hold of a pillow and placed it over my face. I think he was trying to stop me making a noise rather than kill me.'

The terrified old man pretended to fall asleep as his assailant went back into the living room and started searching again. Eventually, the victim did fall asleep and when he awoke at 4.30am his attacker had gone. The lights were not working and neither was the telephone, so he alerted a neighbour who called the police.

A detective constable who arrived at the home at 4.40am said he was met at the front door 'by a frail, elderly male ... he was in a confused, distressed state and he said, "None of my lights are working." I recall him being very tearful and complaining of chest pains.'

Again, the police found that light bulbs had been removed, and again they found that the break-in came via a removed window at the back of the bungalow. In the centre of the lawn was a pane of double-glazed glass, the dew already formed on its underside. Alongside it was the beading that had been removed so the glass could be slipped out from its frame. The police also discovered tool marks on the beading that showed a similarity to the ones found at the homes of several other Stalker victims.

The old man was taken to the Mayday Hospital at Croydon, where a medical examination found bruises to his chest and ribs, and on the upper part of both arms where he had been held tightly. He was so distressed at his ordeal that he could not give a statement to police about the attack, the overall picture being assembled from remarks he made to officers in its aftermath.

But his grown-up son was later to movingly relate the impact the night had had on his father and all their family. Up until his mother's death in 1992, the son said, his father had been 'very quiet and didn't talk much. I remember my father saying "Yes, dear" a lot ... When my mother died, I got closer to my father. He was usually cheerful but quiet. I would visit him every other weekend. While with him we wouldn't talk much – he was never one for sharing his emotions. I would say he was an introvert.

'He was normally quite docile and sweet, but he had another side to him. The only time I remember seeing my father show negative emotion was at his workplace ... I was there one day and I saw him shout at one of his colleagues. It must have taken something really serious for him to get that upset.

'I would cook for him, help him shave, cut his toenails, read short stories to him and frequently we would go for walks around the block until he started getting weaker. He was a creature of habit and he only had a few close friends ... At some point he was diagnosed with Parkinson's Disease and about five years before the incident his sight started going. He had to give up driving because he couldn't see details and he couldn't recognise people.

'As his sight deteriorated, his confidence in going out lessened and he became more confident with his immediate surroundings at home. It took him longer to move around and he always sat in the same chair with a special tape machine for the blind and a radio by his side to listen to audio books. Around the same time, he also started to become more forgetful: he didn't have good memory. He liked living in his house and he was very independent.'

About two years before the attack, the man's two sons hired a home help for their father. 'The last time I saw my dad before the incident would have been the weekend before. I used to stay on the Friday and leave on either the Saturday or Sunday. I can't remember when I left the week before.

'I think the police called me on the day. I knew that he was supposed to be in intensive care for the week, so I would have called one of my colleagues to say that I couldn't be in for a few days. Other than that, I can't remember anything about the day.'

The son went on to say that his dad didn't stay at his house after the burglary. 'In fact, I remember that he wouldn't go into his bedroom again, so he went into respite care for weeks. He settled into the home very quickly and really liked the head of the care home. He also met and made friends with a man who was also blind. The fact that he wanted to stay in the home suggested to me that he was afraid to go back to his own home and that he would rather give up his independence and be looked after.

'He was originally supposed to be in the home for a

couple of weeks. This turned into six weeks. My dad decided that he wanted to move into the home permanently.'

The man and his brother collected their father's belongings and sold his home to pay for the care treatment. 'That was quite emotional for us and time-consuming. We took some of Dad's stuff to him so that he was surrounded by familiar things.

'Dad moving into the home prevented me from spending as much time with him as I used to. I couldn't stay over like I used to, but whenever I visited him I still read to him. I noticed that his memory and his attention span had reduced. He would drop off to sleep while I read to him and his attention would wander while I was speaking to him. On the two or three occasions when we went for a walk, the walks were very much shorter. He got tired very quickly. It was almost like he was giving up.

'The incident affected my dad in many ways. Before the burglary, he was happy in his home and comfortable. Because of what happened, he couldn't stay there any more. He was never much of a talker; he never talked to me about what happened. I was very worried about what had happened to him, but I didn't feel I could talk to him about it because I feared it would bring it all back.

'The effects of the incident on my dad became more apparent after he moved into the home. It wasn't so much physical effects; it was more the mental effects. The biggest example of this was when I went to visit him in the home on 2 September 2000. He had just been fed and was lying on his side facing away from me. I noticed some food on his face and tried to wipe it away. He fought me off, throwing his fists around feebly, shouting something like "Get off me! Don't touch me, and get away from me!" His attempts to fight me off were ineffectual.

'It hurt me so much that he thought I was trying to attack him. I kept trying to say, "It's me," and he eventually calmed down. Towards the end of his life, as his memory deteriorated, the attack came back to him, probably because he never talked about it and just kept it all in. He died on 4 September 2000, two days after that incident.'

The son found his own life, too, was being strongly affected by the incident. 'To sum it up, I felt like shit. I had strong headaches, muscle pains and nightmares. I felt a lot of anger and I can remember feeling so utterly exhausted and my head being so full of thoughts that at times I couldn't sleep. I'm sure he would not have gone into the home at that stage if it had not been for the incident.'

Although the son's remarks were made the year after his father was attacked, there was no disguising the fact that he – like so many other relatives of victims – was struggling to come to terms with the effects of being visited by the Night Stalker.

July 1999 was to be a busy month for Delroy Grant. At least two more elderly victims, this time women, were to suffer at his hands.

CHAPTER FIVE

The 82-year-old woman had been up late that night watching television. It wasn't until midnight that she finally decided it was time to go to bed in her detached two-storey home in Addiscombe, Surrey. It wasn't the kind of home usually favoured by Delroy Grant, but anything was fair game.

The old lady turned off the lights in her double bedroom at the front of the house but, as was her habit, kept the curtains open. She liked it that way. 'When I went to bed, I locked up as usual. The next thing I felt was a hand on my face and mouth.'

She snatched the hand away and she remembered then seeing 'this big, black, hooded face'. The frightened woman asked him, 'What do you want?' and he replied, 'Money.' She indicated that he should go to the wardrobe and he did and immediately started going through her

43

possessions. He found her handbag, removed her purse and took some money from it.

After that, he returned to her bedside and placed his head alongside hers. 'Do you want to have sex?' he asked her. She was so shocked, so taken aback by this perverted suggestion that she had to ask him to repeat what he had said. She literally could not believe what she had heard. When he did, she retorted, 'No – certainly not! I am an old woman. It won't do anything for you or me.'

This did not deter him. He forced her legs apart, moved her nightdress up and placed his hand between her legs. She asked him not to hurt her and was to describe his behaviour as 'almost respectful – he was not violent or aggressive'.

His victim asked if she could go to the toilet and he allowed her to. Then he looked in all her rooms, using his torch to enable him to see in the dark. Then he went downstairs, making the old lady follow him, and on the ground floor he took a can of beer from his pocket and began to drink it. She asked him what kind of drink it was and he said, 'Bitter.' Then he put it down on a table in the hall.

As terrifying as the encounter had been, it was to end in a bizarre fashion. 'By now, I was fed up and decided it was time he went,' his victim explained. 'I opened the front door and said something like, "Thank you for not hurting me."'

Grant then shook her by the hand, gently pushed her away from the front door, opened it and walked out into the night, closing the door behind him.

She went to bed and tossed and turned for 30 minutes before deciding to get up and make some tea. No lights were working and she saw by the light from her small torch that the fuses were missing. That really annoyed her. She wanted her tea and she did not know how to replace the fuses, so she contacted a neighbour and the police were called.

The impact on his latest victim was harsh for her, as it had been for all the others, although she tried to handle it in as stoic a manner as possible. 'I used to be in the army when I was younger and went through the war, so I have seen a lot of things in my life. I consider myself to be a fairly strong and independent person and this may be why this incident hasn't affected me like it may have done a different person. The incident doesn't stop me doing anything, but I will never forget it.

'I didn't hear the man come in. I live in an old house which has squeaky floorboards on the landing. I'm awake straight away. I feel very lucky that the man didn't hurt me as he could have done. I think this was because I am a big person. Had I been smaller or weaker, I think he may have hurt me. I never wanted to leave my house because of what happened, as I wasn't going to have to be made to move because of that wretched man. I shall only move house when I am unable to cope with it. I am, however, more aware of being on my own.

'I remember just after it happened my daughter came to stay with me for a few days to make me feel a bit better. I have a lovely family and I just try to forget it.'

If that victim managed to cope remarkably well with the aftermath of her attack, the same could not be said of another 82-year-old woman who also lived in Addiscombe and who was the target of Grant on Wednesday, 29 July 1999. Hers was a truly terrifying night and it left a lingering legacy of pain and fear.

She and her husband had moved into their semi-detached home soon after the Second World War ended. It had an all-glass porch leading to a patio, and a dressing table with cupboards over it that her late husband had built and installed. The living-room door squeaked and she needed to keep it lubricated with regular applications of WD40.

The couple had two children and, by the time her husband died, after more than 30 years together, her daughter had already left the family home. Later, her son was to fly the nest too, which meant that she had been by herself for 17 years on the night that Delroy Grant entered her life. 'I had been happy and secure with my friends, family and grandchildren nearby until July 1999 when I was burgled and raped' was how she was later to describe her experience.

The old lady, who had had two hip operations some years earlier, had recently been sleeping on a folding bed downstairs as it had been hot and her upstairs bedroom, where she normally slept, was too warm for her. At about 10.15pm, she put on her pale, patterned polyester-cotton nightie with three or four buttons on the front. As was her habit, she checked all the windows and doors and left the porch door on its mortise lock before going to bed. She read her Maeve Binchy book for about half an hour, before taking her glasses off and placing them alongside the glass of orange squash she always had to hand in case she felt thirsty during the night.

At one stage, she awoke to go upstairs to use the toilet and came back down again. Then she heard the living-room door creak. She instantly felt panic as she knew she had closed it before retiring for the night. She got up and went into the living room to investigate and a gloved hand was placed over her face. 'I was so frightened I went limp. I thought, "Oh my God!"'

She said to her assailant, 'I am 82 – what do you want with me?' and back came the same reply he had given before and was to repeat for a decade to come: 'Money.' He moved her back towards where she had been sleeping and she showed him her purse. He took some money out of it, two £20 notes and two £10 notes.

Then he pushed her on to the bed. The image of him towering over her as she lay with her face looking upwards, her head over the edge of the bed, would stay with her for the rest of her years. He tried to open the buttons on her nightie, before ripping it open and trying to fondle her breasts. Then he pulled her underwear off.

'He tried to kiss me. I was horrified. I could not believe this was happening.'

His lips were all over hers and he made her take her false teeth out. They were her upper set and he pointed at her lower teeth and told her to take them out too. She said she couldn't, they were her own. Then he indecently assaulted her. 'I just lay there, passive. I did not want to be beaten up.

'It was horrible,' she added. 'I knew what he was doing. He was raping me.'

Later, he whispered to her, 'Don't tell anyone.'

Afterwards, he began to finger her nightie and told her to take it off. She asked why and he replied, 'There may be semen on it.'

The old woman took the nightie off and put on a slip and knickers, and went into the living room where she sat trembling in an armchair. She heard him moving around upstairs so she went to the back door – perhaps there was a chance to escape. But he came down and she had to return to the chair. She was trapped.

Then he made her go upstairs and he supported her as she climbed the staircase. 'I thought he was going to rape me again. I was so frightened I wanted it to end.' Even so, she still had the presence of mind to slip off her engagement ring and hide it under the valance. 'I did not want him to have that,' she said. He asked her for the back-door key and she took it out of the empty mint-sauce jar where she kept it for safety and handed it to him. He asked where her alarm was and she told him it was not working. The old lady then asked him why he had done such an act and he did not reply. Eventually, he said, 'I will never do it again,' and left.

After he had fled, she saw that her nightdress was in a bowl of water in the sink. The reason for this was simple.

In the years since he had begun his attacks, there had been continual progress in the analysis of DNA, and Grant no doubt knew this. He was anxious to minimise the risk to himself by removing as much of his body fluids as he could from anywhere they might be collected and then examined by forensic scientists.

The victim then phoned her son and told him what had happened. 'I do not know how long my ordeal lasted. It seemed forever,' was how she described it.

After Grant was arrested, her son recalled the events of that evening. He lived about two miles from his mother and he was woken by a 4am telephone call in which she said, 'I have been burgled. I have been raped.' He told his wife to telephone the police as he dressed hurriedly, jumped in his car and drove as quickly as he could to his mother's address.

At the scene of the crime, his mother told police how her attacker had made her take her nightdress off as there might have been semen on it, and that he had put it in the sink to soak. 'He made me kiss him and he had big, rubbery lips,' she said.

Her son said, 'She was visibly shaken; she was in a state of shock. I said, "Are you all right?" and she said, "No, not really." He added, 'My mother did not return to the house after that. She lived with the family for a while and then sheltered accommodation.'

The old woman's description of her attacker was as vague as many other of his victims: taller than her (she was 5 feet 1 inch), black but not very dark-skinned, and he had 'blunt' features. He had a balaclava, gloves and torch.

Police found he had entered her home by removing the lower part of a window from its frame. It was found in the garden and the beading that had been loosened so it could be removed had tool marks on it matching those of break-ins already recorded – and those that were still to be committed.

After the attack, her life changed. She was prescribed Valium and did not sleep well. Even when she did manage to sleep, she would awake 'feeling down'.

'This is an incident I try to forget, but I cannot,' she later explained movingly. 'Shortly after I reported this incident to the police, I underwent an examination by a police doctor. This was an unpleasant experience. I had to undergo many tests for various infections. I then had to wait until November 1999 for HIV tests to be done and wait a couple of weeks for the results. This was very worrying because I didn't know if I had contracted any infection.

'I couldn't go back to the house at first. I moved in with my son and his family.' Her son's two children, who had previously had their own rooms, now had to share one to make room for their grandmother in the other. 'I couldn't live at my old home because I thought the man would come back. I didn't feel safe there.

'I thought my house was pretty secure but he still managed to get in. I remember I was scared to go into my old house on my own after it happened. To start with, I had to take my son with me to pick some things up. After a while, I managed to go there alone, but only during the day.

'Even then, I would lock myself in my house and wear my carelock alarm round my neck while I was there because I was scared. I lived at my son's for about ten months in the end and then sold my house. I also stayed at my daughter's house now and then. My son and his wife even considered selling their house and buying one with a granny annexe on it so that we could live together and I would feel safe. My family were prepared to change their lives totally because of what happened and how it had affected me.

'Eventually, I bought myself the flat where I live now. It is a warden-assisted flat where I know people will be around all the time. It took me so long to find somewhere suitable because I did not want to be on the ground floor. This is where the man got in before and I wanted somewhere on the first floor or above. I haven't told anyone where I live now about what happened, as I don't want to be known as the lady who was raped.

'When I lived at my son's house, I used to have nightmares. I used to be woken up by my son telling me that I had been shouting out in my sleep. I have been told that I shouted things like "No! No, don't! I don't like it!" I don't have nightmares now but I make sure I take certain measures. At night I have to leave a light on in the hallway so that there is light in my room. I make sure all the doors and windows are locked. I do this even in the middle of the summer in the heat. I cannot sleep if they are open because I think that he will be able to get back in.'

The old lady was seen by several doctors after the attack. One noted: 'unable to return to her flat, she is going to relatives.' She was seen by a second doctor in September that year and was prescribed anti-depressants. By the following year, 2000, she was being seen by a Parkinson's specialist who said she 'had become increasingly immobile and she had a tremor in her left hand. That doctor noted that this had happened since the rape and the elderly woman had subsequently had a couple of falls because her balance was not so good.

'I was offered counselling,' said the victim, 'but I did not want this because I have my family around me. I also did not want to keep on talking about it and having to relive it all the time.

'Straight after this incident I started shaking. I couldn't stop. I saw the doctor who gave me some Valium. This made me really sleepy so I got it changed. I now take Paroxitin, which I believe is an anti-depressant.

'I have been told that I may have Parkinson's Disease and I believe it was brought on by this incident.'

The unfortunate woman died in 2007, plagued until the end by that night. But Grant's attempt at hiding or removing his DNA by placing the soiled nightdress in a bowl did not work. That, too, left clues for detectives. We shall be examining the DNA links to Grant in greater detail later, but suffice to say a sample was taken – despite the water the dress had been placed in – and it would reveal a match with Grant.

The visit by Delroy Grant to the old lady's home that July night in 1999 had such an effect on his victim that she lived with the horror that it brought until she died eight years later. Sadly, she was not the only who went to her grave suffering from the consequences of Grant's appalling actions and not knowing that one day he would be brought to justice.

CHAPTER SIX

As July turned to August in that long summer of 1999, the Night Stalker was in a frenzy. It is impossible to say which nights he trailed around the streets of south London and when he stayed at home. Only he will ever know. What is certain is that his attacks were coming at such an increased frequency that action had to be taken, and quickly.

On Tuesday, 3 August, an 88-year-old woman was another of his victims. The woman, of Irish-Scottish descent, had lived in her bungalow home, tucked away in a cul-de-sac on the outskirts of Croydon, for 43 years and had been on her own for 24 years since her husband died. The detached home had a 6ft-high wooden fence and a garage that led to the back garden. The front garden required little maintenance because it was crazy-paved. The woman, whose son had left home many years ago, slept in the main bedroom at the front of the home. The décor was classic: double-glazed throughout except for a couple of doors, built-in wardrobes, chandeliers and French windows out to the rear garden.

Wearing a vest and cotton nightdress down to her ankles, the old lady, who had only returned from hospital a few days earlier after receiving in-patient treatment for a week, drew her lounge curtains as the light began to fade and carried out her customary routine of checking that all the doors and windows were locked. The woman, who was hard of hearing, then took out her hearing aid and put it in a box on top of the television. Then, after quickly going to the bathroom, she settled down in bed around 11.45pm.

'The next thing I remember is being shaken by my shoulder.' She looked at the digital clock at her bedside and saw that it said 'three something'. She started to sit up as there was a black male standing by her bed. He was shining a torch in her face as he removed the bulb from her bedside lamp. Her bed quilt was down to her knees but she was holding the sheet up to her chest. 'I was shocked, petrified, dumbstruck. I did not know what to do.'

The man pulled the sheet away from her and grabbed her arm so furiously that he bruised her. He had undone his trouser flies and he laced her hand on his member. She snatched her hand away quickly and, although there was some resistance from him, he did not move it back. 'What would your mother think of you if she could see you now?' the old lady rebuked him. Later she said, 'I was terrified and shocked. I was just staring at his face, paralysed with fear – wondering how long it would go on for.'

The intruder turned his attention away from her and began searching the bedroom before going out of the door, looking at the rest of her home and then leaving.

When the old lady had summoned up the courage and strength to leave her bedroom, she saw that the bungalow had been ransacked. Furniture was tipped up and he'd left drawers out of sideboards and cupboards in his search for money and valuables. She was shocked to see the mess. Normally, her house was clean as a pin: she was a tidy woman who prided herself on keeping it spotless.

The Night Stalker had gained entry by removing a pane of glass in a lounge window at the rear of the house but for once he had neglected to cut the telephone wire, so she was able to call the police. When they arrived, they found her walking around in a distressed state.

The victim could only describe her assailant as thick-set and strong looking, but there was one clue that was to link Delroy Grant to this crime. As has already been mentioned, a previous victim had seen him casually drink from a can of bitter while in her home. During this latest raid, he had also imbibed. His victim did not know when but it was probably on his way out, another 'evening's work' over. He had opened a miniature bottle of Campari that the old lady had in the house and casually drunk it. Then he had put it back down again. This was a man who at a previous raid had washed a victim's nightgown in a bid to remove traces of his DNA, yet here he was so careless as to drink from a small bottle and, in doing so, leave saliva traces around its neck. It was a mistake that he was to pay for, as a DNA sample was taken and was subsequently linked with him years down the line.

The last of the Night Stalker's seven known raids during that summer of mayhem came a mere two days later, on 5 August. His victim was also 88 and lived in a three-bedroom semi-detached bungalow in Orpington.

It had been an ordinary day for the widow, until he brought terror into it. She had risen at 7.30am and at lunchtime she'd had her hair permed, paying with £27.50 from her purse. Her niece arrived mid-afternoon and the woman gave her £20 with which to do some shopping for her. At 6.30pm, the shopping done and delivered, the niece left. The pensioner, who lived alone, then watched television until midnight, when it was time for bed. There had been a storm late that night so she unplugged the television 'as I was worried about the aerial'.

Her 12ft by 14ft bedroom was at the front of the bungalow; she used the smallest bedroom as a sewing room and kept her sewing machine in there. She slept in a single bed – there was no need for anything larger – with floral sheets with matching pillowcases and two cream blankets. There was also a candy-stripe cushion for extra head support. That night, she was wearing a white cotton nightdress that she had made herself. It had a pattern of small flowers on it.

Also in the bedroom was a trolley, from which she could drink her early-morning tea, and a shopping trolley, which she used as a kind of Zimmer frame if she needed to get up in the night. There was also a clock radio and a night-light plugged into the wall.

During the night, she heard a sound but thought it was her neighbour who worked late shifts. Then the story took a familiar, horrible turn. 'All of a sudden, I saw this figure at the end of the bed. He was completely covered in a catsuit.' He was wearing his sickening uniform of balaclava and gloves, and he shone his torch in her face. 'He covered my face and mouth and I felt that I was being smothered. I could not breathe or see. He whispered, "Don't scream, I won't hurt you."'

Yet again came the pitiful questions from a helpless old person. 'What are you doing here? What do you want?'

Back came the inevitable answer: 'Money.' If only that had been all he wanted.

'You won't find any more here,' the old lady replied. 'It's in the living room.' She also told him that she could not walk, but they were wasted words. What did he care about her wellbeing or her physical problems? She needed to take hold of a walking stick and grip it tightly in her trembling hand to aid her movement as he frogmarched her into the living room. In her bag she had some £60 in notes, a photograph of her mother and an old bus pass photograph.

He was not satisfied. He was never satisfied. He grabbed her by the shoulders and pushed her on to the settee. What followed were, even by his bestial standards, disgusting acts on this helpless old woman, ones which were to result in charges of both rape and indecent assault. They were so depraved that the repetition of them is not bearable. Suffice to say that at one stage, after experiencing 'an awful, searing pain', she cried out to him, 'Oh no, not again!' Later, she said, 'He was really brutal. I just wanted him to stop, the pain was awful.'

Grant, his animal lust eventually satiated in the darkness illuminated only by the light of his torch, then went to the bathroom. He returned and threw a towel at her for her to use, then suddenly began to frantically search for something. When she asked what it was, he said, 'My glove!' She found it and threw it towards him. Then he left. Physically, he departed from her life, but he was to stay with her emotionally and mentally for the rest of her days.

The old woman dragged herself on all fours and got into a chair and at 3.37am she managed to alert the Carelink alarm service by pushing a button. Then she noticed that she was covered in blood.

The Carelink operator who received the call that night said, 'I was sceptical at first. I remember her mentioning bleeding and I thought, "How could anyone do this to an old woman?"' He also knew that on occasions the elderly wake from a dream and think they have experienced reality. Nevertheless, he immediately alerted police and ambulance, and the officers who arrived discovered that her nightdress was indeed covered in blood. It also had traces of Grant's DNA on the front, as had one of the brown cushions in the living room that had once been a haven of peace for his victim but had been turned into a torture chamber by his acts.

At hospital, it was discovered that the woman, who had osteoarthritis in her joints, had cuts to her lips and serious injuries to various parts of her anatomy around her waist and hips that required major surgery.

Yet again, Grant had entered the home by removing a window, this time an entire window, from the kitchen and its beading bore marks similar to other offences.

Although the elderly lady, who was later said to have been 'able to lead a largely independent and fulfilling life', was to recover well from her surgery, she had difficulty in adjusting to its physical after-effects. The effect on her mentally was never to go away. She was never to live again in the bungalow where she had experienced such horror; the psychological effects were so great that she moved into sheltered accommodation where she stayed until her death in 2006.

Her niece encapsulated the agony for many of the relatives of those who suffered at Delroy Grant's hands. 'My aunt was really upset and couldn't understand why somebody could come along and totally ruin her life. She had nightmares. Every time she closed her eyes, she could see a hooded black figure. In the end, she wanted to die and for people to leave her alone.'

CHAPTER SEVEN

Tens of thousands of words would eventually be written about Delroy Grant and his victims, but until late 1999 his activities had not attracted publicity or notoriety on a major scale. One of the first indications that this was to change came with a small item in the *Evening Standard*, the evening newspaper for London and the surrounding areas. It read:

'Detectives today released an e-fit of a man believed responsible for 25 sex attacks in south London, including three rapes and one attempted rape. They are also examining video footage of a suspect near the scene of an attack on an 82-year-old woman in August. The officers working on Operation Minstead originally thought the attacker had committed up to 60 burglaries with indecent assault on pensioners and are concentrating on 25 of those. Police appealed today for help in finding a "vital clue", a gold Victorian watch engraved "FMF", which was stolen from an 89-year-old rape victim in 1992.'

By mid-October, those same detectives had turned to one of Britain's newer crime-fighting weapons to help track down the Night Stalker. Geographic profiling analyses the locations of a series of connected crimes to determine the most probable area where the offender might live. Information about the locations of crimes or where crucial evidence was found is fed into the system, which then carries out millions of mathematical calculations to plot a map of where the suspect is most likely to live. This is shown in red and is known as 'the hunting area' and becomes the focus of police activity.

The technique helps police prioritise information in large-scale major crime investigations that often involve hundreds or thousands of suspects and tips. By obtaining some measure of understanding of an offender's geographical habits and tendencies, investigators and profilers learn a great deal about the lifestyle and personality of the culprit. The map would not be able to track the offender to his doorstep, but the hope is that it might narrow a search area down to a few square miles. Although typically used to catch serial killers or serial rapists, it can also be of use in solving arson, bombing, robbery and other major crimes.

Until the late 1990s, British police had employed psychologists, such as the one portrayed in the *Cracker* television series, to form a profile of the perpetrator's personality in an attempt to solve the crime. With this new method, detectives could use a computer program to deduce where the killer or attacker might live. The technique had only been introduced in the UK in June after proving a success in Canada and the United States, but a prototype had been used during the hunt for the Yorkshire Ripper, and detectives believed that, if they had known more about the system, they could have arrested Peter Sutcliffe much earlier.

It was thought that this method of investigation might be so significant that the police appointed a dedicated geographical profiler based at the staff training college at Bramshill, in Hampshire. By the time Operation Minstead began, Detective Sergeant Neil Trainor had already received 23 requests to use the system from police forces across the country. It was now in use in nine major investigations, one of which was Operation Lynx, an investigation into rapes dating back to 1982 in Leicestershire, Yorkshire and Nottinghamshire.

Mr Trainor later explained, in relation to his work in general, 'Geographic profiling doesn't solve crime but focuses the investigation. Our job is to narrow down the area to optimise the chances of finding the individual.'

A profiler's job is to look at things like where and when the crimes took place and who is being targeted, and they also look at the way a crime has been carried out and the different motivations. Looking at this information over a period of time should start to show patterns.

'It's crucial to work out if the offender lives in the area or not,' Mr Trainor explained. 'In most arson cases and all crimes, quite often the offender is local. But how local is local? What we are trying to establish is where the offender lives. Where there's a critical area with a persistent offender, it's a level of crime worth giving whatever support we can give to. We help forces who have been dealing with murder, rape, abduction and critical incidents; incidents serious enough to put a lot of resources into.'

The method had been developed by Detective Inspector Kim Rossmoor of Vancouver police in the early 1980s and first used officially in 1990 in the US and Canada. Mr Rossmoor pointed out that in some crimes police can end up with a list of several thousand suspects. Geographic profiling gives them a starting point from which to narrow down the list. 'This does not take away contact with the public but gives the police a tool to use,' he said. 'It gives them an idea of what pieces of the jigsaw they should look at first.'

By this stage, the Night Stalker investigation had failed to narrow down the number of possible suspects below 200. A source close to Operation Minstead said, 'We have had no positive leads from our press appeals or the e-fit we issued so we are really waiting to see what this profile will throw up.

'We have never used the technique before so don't really know what to expect. When you first hear about it, it sounds a bit fantastic but the longer this guy is out there, the more likely he is to attack again. We have to try everything.'

One of the first victims of the Night Stalker to go

public was an 87-year-old woman in 2000 who spoke of her ordeal at his hands in the hope that it might help catch the man. 'I don't want revenge but I do want him caught,' she said. 'He has attacked vulnerable, elderly women who live alone, which I think is inexcusable.' She had not been sexually attacked but she had endured a terrifying few hours when the man broke into her south-east London home.

In his by-now customary method, he had removed a pane of glass from a French window and crawled inside before confronting her. 'A dark, tall figure came in and put his hand over my mouth. He shoved me on the bed, sat beside me and put his arm around me then whispered the word, "Sex".' He then spent some time searching her house before leaving.

Psychologist Dr Julian Boon, who had provided Scotland Yard with a criminal profile of the attacker, said the attacker was one of a rare group sexually obsessed with old women. 'His primary motive is sexual and having a relationship,' he told BBC Radio 4's *Today* programme. 'That would suggest he has a paraphilia [abnormal sexual behaviour]. We use the word paedophilia for people who have a love of and sexual interest in children; likewise he is something that we call a gerontophile – he has an interest in the elderly.'

Dr Boon – a member of the family who publish Mills and Boon romantic books – was to say in one interview during the hunt for the serial attacker, 'There is a trap here and we mustn't fall into it. When we see what this man has done, the pain he has inflicted on helpless old women, we naturally experience an incredible sense of outrage. We are angry and we see him as a monster. But that could easily hinder the process of trying to identify him because I believe that to the people around him he is not a monster. On the contrary, I suspect he is someone who is well liked, even admired, for being caring and kind.'

Dr Boon, often referred to as a real-life Cracker, had been to many of the Night Stalker's crime scenes. 'It was vital for me to go to every house. I wanted to see what we call the "stimulus array" – what he was seeing. I realised he had picked houses of a certain type – they all had places from which he could secretly observe the person inside. The evidence shows he would spend large amounts of time just watching ... watching the old lady make a cup of tea, moving around, getting ready for bed. We know that when he got inside he would go from room to room, looking at things, opening drawers and cupboards, examining, observing. He did steal some stuff but not much. The real purpose was to get into the life of his victim. He would look out of their windows, take in the scenes they saw every day.

'Don't misinterpret what I'm going to say because I hold no brief for this man and I am as outraged about his crimes as everyone else, but I can't let anger cloud my judgement. I think he is not just a depraved beast. I believe he does not want to hurt his victims. I think he wants a relationship with them.'

The Night Stalker, Dr Boon said, was a gerontophile, someone who is erotically attracted to elderly people.

'If we look at how he behaves, we see a pattern that shows he is not a typical rapist. He doesn't grab them and shout, "Get your knickers off or I'll kill you!" He doesn't grab them by the throat and he doesn't beat them. On the contrary, when he has been beaten by them, with a stick or whatever, he has not retaliated. He has simply put up a hand to protect himself. What this tells us is crucial – he doesn't want to hurt them. Yes, of course he has caused incredible pain and suffering, but I believe he has regretted that afterwards.'

Dr Boon pointed out that after one particularly appalling rape – of an 89-year-old woman in Shirley in 1992 – the attacks stopped for five years. After the rape of an 88-year-old woman in 1999, he did not strike again for two years.

'I think he tried to stop when he realised what he'd done but he can't stop. He's getting something he craves out of it. This man is looking for romantic love. He would like nothing more than to strike up a relationship with one of his victims and settle down into a life as a couple.' Dr Boon based this theory on evidence from victims. 'In a number of cases, the rapist has spent long periods talking to the women about themselves and their life. He has behaved tenderly towards them – and even responded to their pleas to leave them alone. Where he has carried out sexual assaults or rape, he has in several cases attempted to minimise the distress of his victims, lifting one into a position that caused least pain.'

Dr Boon said the Night Stalker used 'finesse' in his crimes. 'He is meticulous in the way he breaks into the houses. He removes glass panes, uses tools. He doesn't just smash in doors or windows. He could be a tradesman, or someone who works with their hands. The most obvious thought is that he works with old people. Like paedophiles, who like to work with children, gerontophiles gravitate towards jobs caring for the elderly. I am sure he will not appear to be a sadistic beast to people who know him but probably someone quite kind and gentle.'

According to experts on gerontophilia, the Night Stalker probably had an erotic experience involving an elderly person at a crucial stage in his childhood. It may have been seeing someone undress, or it might have been a close relationship with a foster parent. 'We cannot re-wire his head,' Dr Boon said. 'He has to be caught and stopped – he cannot stop himself.'

By November 2000, police had quadrupled the number of officers hunting the Night Stalker and were planning to possibly carry out DNA tests on more than 2,000 men. Officers had already started a mass screening of young black males with criminal records amid fears the attacker would strike over the festive period as he had done before. He had committed a cluster of attacks around the Christmas break in 1998.

In the eight years that had passed since that first attack in 1992, police said four victims had been raped and numerous others sexually abused, as well as an estimated

66 burglaries carried out. His victims were mainly women in their eighties, but included two in their nineties, and his last attack had been carried out on 21 April when an 87-year-old woman had been attacked in the Shortlands district of Bromley.

A Scotland Yard spokesman said there were now 26 officers dedicated solely to catching the attacker and 1,400 of the 2,000 DNA samples had already been taken. 'We believe that the net is now closing in on this man,' a police spokesman said – somewhat optimistically as it transpired – but added that known criminals were also cooperating. 'It is not only the public which is disgusted by these acts but also criminals who are coming forward to help us.'

The net may have been 'closing in' but it was still a long way from trapping the Stalker when, in April 2001, the Minstead team turned to other members of the police force for help. More than 720 videos about the horrific crimes were released and distributed to London police stations. The video, narrated by Nick Ross of *Crimewatch*, was handed to every police station in London with instructions to borough commanders to make sure all officers watched it.

Detective Chief Inspector David Zinzan said, 'I believe a police officer knows who this man is. It is likely this man has come into contact with the police in the past. They may have had him in the charge room at some point on an apparently unconnected incident which, having seen the video, bears the hallmarks of crimes committed by this man. Police officers might have been transferred to different stations so we're urging those who worked in Lewisham, Bromley, Croydon and Bexley stations to watch the video carefully.'

The winter of 2002 marked the tenth anniversary of the first 'known' attack of the Stalker, and police feared that he might mark it with a renewed spate of attacks. They were to be proved right. One of them, on a 77-year-old in Shirley on 13 October, was particularly gruesome. We will deal in detail with the events of that night in due course, but suffice to say it meant police were on full alert for his next strike.

Detective Chief Inspector Simon Morgan said, 'The suspect undoubtedly has home or work connections in Croydon or in the Bromley borough, where he has struck at least five times. The man's behaviour suggests he is in need of help and care. He responds to his victims' mood and any mention of his family causes him to stop.'

One criminal psychologist said, 'The man is more than likely to have been abused by his father, or an older brother. He will have had a disturbed early childhood and adolescence. He will be unforgiving of his father, or whoever inflicted the abuse, which would be sexual or severe psychological torment. It may well have been hidden from his mother until she was forced to face up to it. He will feel ambivalent to his mother and possibly feel she should have done something about it. I do not think this guy's sole intention is to get a sexual buzz – it's more about inflicting terror and psychological abuse by using sex as a weapon.'

By February 2003, uniformed officers and detectives from the South London Metropolitan Police Serious Crime Group were handing out leaflets to motorists and pedestrians in Shirley offering a £10,000 reward for information leading to the conviction of the suspect.

Mr Morgan was quoted as saying, 'We are investigating 26 linked incidents, which have occurred in south London since October 1992. The last incident occurred in Shirley during the early hours of Sunday, 13 October 2002. On that occasion, the suspect was wearing dark clothing, possibly an all-in-one tracksuit, a baseball cap and gloves. On previous occasions, he has been known to wear a balaclava. The suspect knows what he is doing is wrong and we believe he needs help. I would ask him, how would you feel if someone did this to your mother or a member of your family?'

In March 2003, the Night Stalker struck again, his first known attack since the one in October. In the early hours of a Saturday morning, he broke into a 78-year-old woman's home on the Kingswood estate in south east London. The pensioner fought him off, suffering injuries to her face, but he escaped with her jewellery, including a diamond engagement ring and two gold bracelets.

Police believed he might also have been behind a break-in at a pensioner's home in Catford three days earlier in which £300 was taken but there was no sexual attack. Detectives feared that he had begun to offend again after a gap of several months, and in April 2003 senior detectives from Operation Minstead called a public meeting in Orpington. The public briefing was to reassure residents and tell them that more than 50 Serious Crime Unit officers would be carrying out house-to-house enquiries within a half-mile radius. Mr Morgan said, 'He either lives, works or has some connection with someone he visits in Orpington. This could be a child, a school or a job. We want people to come forward and tell us if they know of anyone who matches the description. Three of his victims have gone to their grave not knowing who their attacker is and we are determined to catch him. We believe he is sorry for what he does and he can get help for his condition.'

The Operation Minstead team had spent years scouring records, including DNA databases, from all over the world and had eliminated more than 16,500 people from its enquiries.

At this stage, the total number of victims was estimated to be at least 80 elderly women across south London over the previous decade, 26 of whom had also been sexually assaulted, either raped or indecently assaulted. Seven of the offences had been linked by DNA and the remainder through the methods of the attacker. Many of the attacks had taken place within a mile and a half of each other in the Shirley area of Croydon and detectives believed the suspect might live or work there. His description also included having a south London accent.

Yet again, Mr Morgan spoke of the need to catch the

attacker. 'Criminal profilers have told us that he has been able to control his urges. There have been gaps where that has happened but then it starts again. Three victims have gone to their graves not knowing who this man was or why this happened to them.'

Mr Morgan added that the man was meticulous in planning his attacks and his victims were often too frightened to call police. 'We think the identity of the suspect will be a surprise to everyone. I don't think even his closest family will suspect him.' Police had spoken to convicted rapists with a similar compulsion to abuse elderly people, and had even found one man who took his wife and children on trips to research future victims. 'I think this man must know that he needs help,' Mr Morgan added, 'and I would urge him to come forward voluntarily.'

Addressing the Stalker directly, Mr Morgan said, 'You know what you're doing is wrong. We believe you need help. How would you feel if someone did this to your mother or a member of your family?'

On Monday, 9 June, an 84-year-old woman from West Croydon was pushed on to her bed and smothered with a pillow while the suspect demanded money. He escaped with cash and credit cards. That night, the man also broke into the home of a 75-year-old woman in Addiscombe, stealing £20 cash. Saturday, 23 August saw the Stalker threaten to rape a 66-year-old woman from Kendra Hall Road, South Croydon before indecently touching her. He stole £30 cash and escaped.

Dr Boon again delivered his verdict on the attacker. 'I

was called in to create a profile of this man to help the police. This is a man who has been profiled as a gerontophile, a man who loves older women. It is likely that sometime in the past or late childhood he has been attracted sexually to an older woman, or had some experience where he's become sexually attracted to an older woman in the past. It's very likely that he feels he loves his victims and would very much like to have a normal relationship with them. However, these women are unlikely to want that kind of relationship or attention. There's little other avenue for him. He's probably unaware that he's causing them harm by his actions. In fact, it would probably shock and distress him to discover that he's having such a terrible effect on them.'

Dr Boon also tried to explain the long gaps between attacks. 'It's possible that something that happened when he attacked a woman in 1992 made him think again. But this behaviour is now wired into him.

'Like paedophiles often make a beeline for jobs that involve children, it is possible this man works with the elderly. But this doesn't mean to say that all people who want to work with children are paedophiles.

'It's important for people not to panic but they should be vigilant.'

In September 2003, Scotland Yard issued another appeal for help in catching the Night Stalker through the BBC *Crimewatch* programme. Presenter Nick Ross too made a direct appeal to the Stalker telling the man he was 'in the grip of a compulsion' and urged him to give himself up as more details of the 2003 attacks became public. One development that the broadcast mentioned, and which would subsequently be discussed at Delroy Grant's trial, was the discovery of a size 10 Nike training shoe imprint at the scene of one of his crimes.

In November, a newspaper doubled the £10,000 reward on offer, and Mr Morgan, in an interview to coincide with that news, further expanded on the behaviour of the man he was hunting. 'Every offence involves a burglary. We believe this man walks the streets looking for victims then strikes between midnight and 4am, wearing a black catsuit, gloves and a balaclava with slits for eyeholes. He gains entry through a window, carefully removing the pane of glass in one piece. He then cuts the phone and electricity wires before creeping into the bedroom and waking his victim with the torch. He usually stays several hours, walking the victim round the house and speaking in whispers. It's an utterly terrifying experience for the women.'

Police thinking at that time was that the attacker might have relatives in Orpington, Kent, as he had struck there on a Boxing Day. He had targeted the Shirley, Coulsdon, Forest Hill, Dulwich, Sidcup and Catford areas of south London. There had been gaps in his reign of terror – October 1992 to 1996, and August 1999 to October 2002 – which, the theories went, might match prison sentences or trips abroad.

'We need people to think who he might be,' added Mr Morgan. 'Do you know anyone who goes out late?

Someone with an unhealthy interest in elderly ladies? This man will carry on until he's stopped. We have to take him off the streets.'

The clues at that time were as follows: 'The man was black with a light skin tone, 30 to 40, medium build and wears size 10 shoes. He might work in an old folks' home or day centre and have relatives in Orpington, Kent. The date 13 October could have special meaning for him – he has attacked twice on that day.'

It wasn't much to go on, and the chances were that after all these years it would not be enough.

CHAPTER EIGHT

Although one of the Night Stalker's victims had gone public in 2000, none had yet spoken at length about their ordeal. Then, in July 2004, a 93-year-old woman revealed exactly what it felt like to be attacked and brutalised by the monster. We have already touched upon her case, but the dramatic recounting of the twice-widowed pensioner's ordeal added greatly to the insight the world at large had about his deeds.

The woman, who was identified only by a pseudonym, lived in a three-bedroomed bungalow in a pleasant part of Orpington, Kent. 'I loved it there,' she told *The Times* newspaper five years after the attack, by which time she was living at an old folks' home. 'I remember it very clearly. I'd had my hair done in the morning, someone had done my shopping for me in the afternoon and there was a storm in the evening.

'At about 11pm I heard someone moving around, a noise I thought was my next-door neighbour, a shift worker, coming home. I had unplugged my television in the living room because of the storm and I was in bed watching TV there. I thought my neighbour was being unusually noisy – then I heard a sound in the hallway and the next thing I knew there was a hooded man at the foot of my bed. I remember being very calm. I just said to him, "What are you doing here? What do you want?" He just whispered, "Money", and I told him he wouldn't find any here.

'Then he put two hands around my neck and said, "Don't scream and you won't be hurt." He pulled me out of bed and frogmarched me down the hall and into the living room and threw me into my big armchair. My bag was there and I gave him my purse. He took it. There was £60 or £70 inside. And the next thing I knew I was being assaulted. I remember screaming and then I must have passed out.

'I had already been assaulted once and I remember thinking in the dark that I must have had an accident and wet myself. He was using a torch and went into my bathroom and brought a towel back and threw it at me to dry myself. Then he came at me again. I said, "No, please! Can't you go and get a prostitute? Why pick on old ladies of 88?" But he did it again.

'Afterwards, I was lying there and he started marching round the living room lifting up cushions. I thought he was going to smother me. I asked what he was looking for and he said. "A glove." Then I felt it next to me and threw it on the floor. "There's your glove," I said. "Now get out!" He went into my kitchen and I heard him washing something. Then it went quiet.

'I just lay there for ages not knowing if he was still in the bungalow, and eventually I crawled to the phone but it was dead. He had cut the line. So I crawled to my Carelink alarm and pressed the button. Eventually, an ambulance and the police came and I heard someone calling me. I managed to crawl to the front door to let them in and then I was just invaded by police.

'It was then that I realised I hadn't wet myself. It was blood. If I hadn't had that alarm, I would have bled to death by the morning. It was now 3am. Four hours had passed since he first got in. I hadn't heard him leave because he had gone through the window – he had taken out the entire window frame.'

The woman was rushed to hospital where she was sedated, as it was not possible to operate on her immediately because of the condition she was in.

'The next day, they operated on my bowel and bladder. I had suffered terrible internal injuries. I have a vague memory of people coming and going, visiting me, but I was unconscious from the Friday, when they operated, until the Sunday. When I woke up, I found they'd put a colostomy bag on my stomach. I was in hospital for a month, then a nursing home for two months until I had recovered enough for them to reverse the colostomy operation in the October. I was in hospital 11 days that time.

'That man did awful things to me. And I still have terrible mental and psychological scars to show for it. This man has taken my life away from me. I still have nightmares about what happened. For months I was terrified he could have passed on a disease to me. I have lost my peace of mind, my home and my independence.

'I know people have difficulty in confronting what this pervert is doing. People don't like to talk about it, but they must think what they can do to help the police. Someone out there must suspect someone. Someone might even be protecting him – look what state he must have been in after he raped me. But he must be caught before he does this to someone else. I wouldn't want anyone to experience what I went through.'

Dr Julian Boon was again quoted on the subject of her attacker. 'A gerontophile is someone who feels a real sexual attraction to old people – people in their seventies, eighties or nineties. We simply don't know how prevalent gerontophilia is because most people who had such feelings would simply compartmentalise them and put them away. They wouldn't act upon them. But this man has crossed the line.

'Imagine if you were at a bus stop and saw a very attractive young woman in the queue. The feelings of attraction a sexually normal man might experience towards her are exactly the same as a gerontophile might experience if he saw an old woman with a Zimmer frame. We are genetically programmed against such feelings because the rules of natural selection would have determined that in the early days of man anyone feeling such an attraction would have had nothing to contribute to the next generation. They would not have been able to pass on their genes with an old woman. They would have died out.

'One thing that is certain from what we know of the Minstead attacks is that the man here really loves old women. In the conversations he has had, it is quite clear that he not only finds them sexually attractive, but he would also love nothing more than to establish a real relationship with his victims. He actually has no intention of hurting them. And in the instances when he has hurt victims badly, there have been long periods when he has arrested his behaviour and not attacked again. He has clearly experienced deep feelings of self-disgust and regret. He doesn't hate these women; he wants to love them.'

Detectives hunting the attacker believed then, as they did throughout their inquiry, that many elderly women whom the Stalker had burgled or physically assaulted were too upset to report the matter or, if they or their relatives did contact police, they were too embarrassed to mention the sexual element of the raids.

Meanwhile guidelines were issued to the public to help keep the Night Stalker at bay:

- Buy a panic alarm that should be kept near your bed or around your neck.
- Have someone install sensor lights at the back and side of your home.

- Put locks on toolsheds or keep tools indoors.
  Minstead man has used people's own tools in
  previous attacks.
- Younger neighbours should be aware of the
  dangers and keep a special eye on older people in
  their street.
- If you see anyone in your back garden dial 999
  immediately.
- Report anyone who appears to be taking an
  unusual interest in houses in your street – especially
  if you know an elderly person lives there.

By the spring of 2004, DNA markers and available
descriptions had left detectives with more than 20,000
potential suspects, so cutting-edge advances in DNA
profiling were being used to narrow down the numbers.
As one detective on the case said, 'There are obvious
ethical difficulties in knocking on the doors of 20,000
people and asking them for a DNA sample. The new
methods, using mitochondrial DNA markers on the
female side, and Y-chromosome markers on the male side,
can provide detailed ancestral clues as to the origins of a
person's family.'

The new procedure of ancestral testing – similar to
'familial testing' – was to give detectives their biggest lead
yet in tracing the attacker. Familial searching is the use of
family members' DNA to identify a closely related suspect
in jurisdictions where large DNA databases exist, but no
exact match has been found.

A couple of months earlier, in April 2004, the case of Craig Harman was thought to have been the first in the world in which familial searching had helped bring a killer to justice. Harman, a 20-year-old man, had hurled a brick from a motorway bridge, killing a lorry driver, Michael Little, 53. Harman admitted the manslaughter but conceded his guilt only when confronted with the scientific evidence six months after Mr Little's death.

Harman, a sports-shop assistant who lived with his girlfriend in Frimley, Surrey, had been out drinking with friends in nearby Camberley. He'd cut his hand while breaking into a car, then he and a friend had picked up a couple of bricks from a garden. When they crossed a motorway footbridge, they threw them on to the road. Harman, who said he was 'fairly drunk' after nine or more pints of lager and 'acting like an idiot', said he had meant to annoy drivers and interfere with the flow of traffic.

The brick, with his blood on it, was found in the lorry's cab but did not match anything on the national DNA database because Harman had no previous convictions. After consulting the Forensic Science Service, Surrey police used familial searching. They found that the blood on the brick matched that of a close relative of Harman, who did have a criminal conviction and was on the database, by 16 points out of 20. They then traced Harman, who was eventually jailed for six years at the Old Bailey.

Using DNA recovered from the scene of the Night Stalker's assaults, Operation Minstead detectives now used familial DNA searching to determine if any of the attacker's relatives were on the national DNA database. They also attempted to narrow down his ethnic origin – ancestral as opposed to familial testing, which had not been used in the UK before.

The Minstead team, working with Professor Paul McKeigue, a genetic epidemiologist at University College, Dublin, sent the Stalker's DNA for analysis to DNAPrint Genomics in Florida, a company involved in mapping the human genome. After breaking it down into 177 different parts or 'markers', some of which indicated his ancestry, they established that the rapist's ancestry was 82 per cent sub-Saharan, 12 per cent Native American and 6 per cent European, with a few uncertain percentage points. That was a combination found only in the Caribbean, a region that had been colonised by North American Indians, who were succeeded by European colonists and their slaves.

The detectives now felt that the attacker was a black man originally from the West Indies. Mr Morgan said, 'After 12 years, we feel this is a major breakthrough and are confident that the new DNA results should lead us to the suspect or even his relatives. We have travelled all over the world comparing DNA samples and databases without success but we believe that the scientific advancements will allow us to discover exactly which island in the West Indies the suspect's ancestors are from and even what town.'

Mr Morgan, who said it was a 'miracle' that none of the Night Stalker's victims had died of fright, added, 'This man is a ruthless individual who preys on the most vulnerable members of society. He has been very careful. He has never selected a house which has a younger member of the family living there.

'He often spends a considerable time in the house, which is unusual for a burglar. We believe this is because he enjoys the domesticity of being with elderly people. It's in the dark. He shines a torch in their face; the descriptions that you get are very limited. The victims are petrified. I've met all of the 31 victims. Unfortunately, three have gone to their graves not knowing who he was and why he picked them.

'Anything that gives us more information about this man or allows us to build up a picture of him means it's more likely someone will recognise him. I would ask members of the public who do think they have information or might know the identity to report it. I would reassure anyone who suspects someone but is worried the person might be innocent that we have very good forensic evidence that will allow us to discount them if they are innocent.'

The Minstead team now wanted to conduct voluntary tests on up to 200 male and female Scotland Yard staff who also originated from the Caribbean, to be stored on no other crime database. Detectives wanted to compare their DNA and family history with the suspect's to identify which island, or even town, he came from.

All did not go smoothly, however. In May 2004, the *Daily Mail* reported, 'The hunt for Britain's most prolific serial sex attacker is being thwarted by political correctness in the police force, it emerged last night. Detectives had hoped to catch the so-called Night Stalker by pinpointing his Caribbean origins using revolutionary DNA analysis.

'For the method to work, they wanted to carry out voluntary tests on Scotland Yard staff who originate from the West Indies. Their aim was to compare their DNA and family history with the suspect's to identify which island, or even town, he comes from. Now in a major setback to their 12-year investigation, they have been banned from taking samples after a warning about race "sensitivity" from the Black Police Association.'

The paper added that one of the 50 officers who had offered to provide a sample and give details of their family origins said, 'We wanted to help and now we've been told that we can't. It's political correctness gone crazy.'

'This [DNA sampling] would be unusually reliable because the volunteers were serving police officers with no reason to disguise their backgrounds. It is understood that detectives were particularly anxious for the samples to be given as soon as possible because the Night Stalker is known to favour summer attacks.

'Following a meeting with the BPA executive, its Metropolitan branch complained that the procedure did not apply to white officers. Then, acting on legal advice, senior officers at the Yard decided they did not want to go ahead without BPA backing. So when volunteers turned up to give DNA swabs, they were told they could not take part.

'One officer was quoted as saying: "We were really keen to help. We are astonished that the Association intervened. We don't see this as offensive, sensitive or racist in any way." Another, whose grandmother came to Britain from the Caribbean three generations ago, said: "It was a unique opportunity for ordinary police officers to help bring the perpetrator of some seriously sick crimes to justice. If they had wanted to take samples from white officers, the DNA lab would already have those samples, no question."

'The restriction on using the police officers' DNA caused "extreme frustration" among detectives involved in the Night Stalker inquiry,' a senior source told the *Daily Mail*. He added, 'We cannot believe anyone would try to impede the investigation in this way. It is not helpful and it does the Association's reputation no good whatsoever.'

Chief Inspector Leroy Logan, who chaired the Met's BPA, denied it had instructed members not to cooperate, the paper added, and insisted that individuals were free to do so if they wished. He said, 'We didn't feel comfortable being seen as taking a lead on this. But we didn't make the decision to call it off. It was the powers that be who were calling the shots.'

A Scotland Yard spokesman said, 'We are in negotiation with the BPA and other staff associations.'

The attempt to carry out the DNA testing on black police staff caused more discussion when the next month the *Guardian* reported that: 'Scotland Yard has been accused of sending threatening letters to men who have refused to supply them with samples of their DNA as part of a long investigation to catch a rapist.

'The force has been asked to justify its tactics after suggesting to black men in south London that their failure to submit to voluntary DNA tests is hampering the investigation, one of the largest ever undertaken by the Met.'

The newspaper reported that a senior detective said in the letter: 'Consider that the suspect is likely to refuse to provide a voluntary sample; catching him will be far easier if he is the only one. I will be reviewing the circumstances surrounding your refusal and will notify you of my decision. In the meantime I would ask you to reconsider the request.'

One Metropolitan Police Authority member said, 'The letter is intimidatory. If you are asking for people's cooperation and support, how can you send them this letter? The two things don't marry up.'

The debate, however, continued that summer when *The Times* revealed that five male members of the public had been forced to give DNA samples to police, in breach of Home Office guidance, as part of a criminal investigation.

'The five were arrested and compelled to provide DNA after refusing voluntarily to give samples in the hunt for the attacker and the samples will be stored permanently on the new national database of DNA taken from suspects who have been arrested. The move raised concerns that it will be impossible for anyone to refuse to give DNA samples to police in the future,' the paper said.

'The tests were supposed to be voluntary and the Yard denied that any arrests had been made.

'Ms Lynne Featherstone, a member of the Metropolitan Police Authority [and future MP] said she had been shown letters sent to the men which she says are intimidatory.'

'When she questioned Sir Ian Blair, the then deputy commissioner of the Metropolitan Police, about the use of the tests, he wrote to her saying that there had been 125 initial refusals and the police "had only used powers of arrest five times". [This was later officially reduced to four.] Ms Featherstone said she was concerned at the effects of the intimidation and arrests on the black community and the use of the "intimidation and the arrests was insensitive".

'"This kind of intimidation is exactly the opposite of what should be happening. It not only jeopardises finding the criminal, it also damages the fragile relationship between the police and the community."'

The Black Police Association said the organisation had been consulted on elements of the investigation but not the DNA trawl. 'We know this is a horrendous case, but the use of such strong-arm tactics is a big issue.'

The Times added that, according to the Home Office, the powers that give police the authorisation to take DNA samples could only be used on the grounds that they have a reasonable basis for suspecting that the individual committed the crime.

Home Office sources told the paper that police could not reasonably say that all five of the men arrested could be suspects. A spokesman said, 'I don't think this has ever been tested in the courts. If the DNA had been taken on arrest, it was automatically added to a national database even if you are cleared. If it was given voluntarily, it can be kept but only with written consent.'

Some 120 people had refused to provide DNA, the paper reported, prompting police to send letters asking them to reconsider. 'Those who continued to refuse have been arrested and compelled to give a sample. The controversial programme in which black police officers were asked to give their DNA to help further to isolate the suspect's origins has also resumed after being briefly suspended.'

(The question of DNA research and the testing of both Met. staff and members of the public was to be examined in a report into Operation Minstead by the Metropolitan Police Authority, which we deal with in detail in a later chapter.)

Whether the Night Stalker read these reports we will probably never know. One thing was certain, however, he was soon to be back in business.

CHAPTER NINE

The Night Stalker seemed to be a man whose attacks came in waves, and by the late summer of 2004 he was going about his business again. Early in the morning of 7 September, a burglary in Bromley, Kent, right in the heart of his hunting ground, had all the trademarks of his assaults. Although the occupant, a woman in her eighties, was not a victim of a sexual assault this time, she had been left 'traumatised' by the break-in.

As autumn turned to winter, three more offences were reported. On 18 September, an 84-year-old woman in Grove Park, Bromley, had her home broken into and £1,000 stolen. The old lady, a grandmother, kept him talking for almost four hours before he left. Exactly one month later on 18 October, an 81-year-old woman suffered a sexually motivated attack at her home in Welling, Kent. In this incident, he took out all the light bulbs and spent hours talking to the elderly woman before escaping empty-handed after she'd begged him to leave her alone. Then, on 20 November, an 80-year-old man in West Wickham, Croydon, had his house broken into by a raider wearing a balaclava and black catsuit. Again, he left, without committing a sexual assault, after speaking to the victim for several hours.

One senior detective said, 'I'd urge everyone to be extra vigilant over Christmas. We are determined to get him before another horrific attack.'

He was right to warn of more attacks. In the early part of January 2005, the Night Stalker broke into the home of an 82-year-old woman living alone in Sanderstead in Croydon, and stole cash and valuables. He did not assault her and she was unharmed by the burglary, although shaken by it, as all his victims were. It was impossible to put an exact figure on his raids, but by common agreement this was his 95th offence; the tally was growing at a remarkable rate.

Again, Operation Minstead and the hunt for the Stalker featured on BBC's *Crimewatch*, its third appearance, on 23 February. A number of attacks on women in their eighties in south east London were re-created in graphic, chilling style and, after the programme was broadcast, police received 67 calls and more were made directly to the show itself. 'Following the *Crimewatch UK* appeal, a significant number of calls have generated positive lines of enquiry,' a police spokesman said. 'Operation Minstead officers will be following them up.'

Positive lines or not, the trail went cold and the Stalker disappeared again. But, by October 2006, it was necessary for the police to renew their publicity campaign as his total of known or suspected crimes inched towards the 100 mark. During this fresh appeal at New Scotland Yard, Det. Supt. Morgan revealed that the sex attacker had also targeted four men, and indecently assaulted one of them.

Mr Morgan also revealed that detectives believed the attacker had a conscience, from the way he had responded to his victims' pleas. Evidence also pointed to a possible knowledge of religion. On one occasion, the rapist had declined to take money intended for a church collection. But on another he had stolen rosary beads – one of a number of unusual ornaments he had taken from his victims, possibly as mementos.

Speaking directly to the man, Mr Morgan said, 'In 1999, you raped an 88-year-old lady and she suffered a perforated bowel. Very sadly, she died only recently but she lived the last of her years in absolute agony because of what you did. You know that this has to stop and you know that you have to come forward and hand yourself in to police.'

Pressed on the question of whether police believed the attacker had a conscience, Mr Morgan said, 'Absolutely. He does have a conscience – we've seen that from the way that he has behaved when victims have challenged him. He knows this is wrong, and he knows that it has to stop and it will stop and he has to come forward.'

Analysis of the attacks showed a series of clustered incidents between 1990 and 1992, 1996 and 2000, and 2002 and 2005, with gaps in between when he might have been out of the country. Attacks had been concentrated, police said, particularly around the end of September and month of October, a period thought to be a possible 'trigger'. Police also believed that the man may have been walking the streets looking for potential victims. Mr Morgan said he showed a good knowledge of the areas where his attacks had been concentrated, including knowledge of back streets.

Highlighting that a £40,000 reward was by now on offer for information leading to the attacker's arrest and conviction, Mr Morgan issued a plea to the public. 'Think very laterally. If there is anybody that you suspect who fits these characteristics and criteria we have mentioned, then please contact us. Innocent people can be and will be eliminated.'

Later, at a news conference at Brighton's John Street police station, Mr Morgan said the attacker had mentioned Brighton to his victims consistently over a number of years. Mr Morgan added that police were keeping an open mind about whether he lived, worked or had family in the East Sussex city. Again, Mr Morgan added that the offender was not on the DNA database but stressed it would be simple to clear those unconnected with the offences.

But soon the focus of the investigation would switch to the other side of the Atlantic, and it was revealed that detectives would be heading to the Caribbean in an attempt to trace the Stalker. Detectives suspected he might have gone there in lulls between spates of attacks, and planned to fly out to liaise with police there and make a public appeal to islanders for information.

'The purpose of our visit is to try to narrow down our list of possible suspects by using the very latest forensic techniques,' said Mr Morgan. 'We believe there may be links down the generations between our suspect and countries of the Caribbean. We know the offender has periods of non-offending that may suggest he is not always in the UK.'

On 7 September 2006, the Metropolitan Police Authority produced a report called *The Use of DNA in Operation Minstead*. It is worth noting its contents in detail, not just for the obvious relevance indicated by its title, but for an overall view of where the inquiry stood at that stage. It read:

'Summary: Operation Minstead is the largest hunt for a serial rapist that Scotland Yard has ever mounted and was established in 1997 following the forensic link of two rape offences. The first confirmed offence was in 1992, the second offence being linked initially in 1997. Since the enquiry was established, work has continued to review all other similar offences going back to 1990, which is the earliest offence that can be linked to this series. As a consequence, a total of 97 offences have now been linked.

This linking falls into three categories, definite DNA, other forensic comparisons and methodology. These offences include a series in the summer of 2003 and more recently in the autumn of 2004. The last offence attributed to this offender was on 7 February 2005. Therefore, from the police and community perspective, this remains a significant inquiry to catch a dangerous predatory offender.'

The report continued:

'What we know about the offender:

1. Given the known demographics of this individual from interviews of witnesses and the use of behavioural profiling, we can deduce the following facts. The offender was around the age of 20–21 when he first began this series of offences, which will make him aged around 37 at this time. We cannot rule out the possibility of further offences having been committed prior to this identified series but data does not exist at this time to make any more conclusive linkage nationally. The behavioural science reports strongly indicate that this man will continue to offend until caught. This type of offender is extremely rare and is categorised as a gerontophile (one who seeks sexual gratification from the elderly).

2. The suspect operates in a wide area of south London and identifies single elderly women living alone and, on occasions, lone males. He breaks into properties during the early hours, often removing whole double-

glazed units to gain entry. His modus operandi is one of meticulous preparation, pre and post offence. The telephone is disabled, either cut or pulled from sockets. The electricity is switched off at the mains or he removes fuses. Light bulbs are removed and curtains drawn. Tools to gain entry are often taken from nearby garden sheds. The suspect often wears a mask and gloves. Victims are awoken by shining a torch in their eyes. The offender spends considerable time with the victim, up to four hours in one instance. So far he has left his DNA at ten scenes with another 11 being linked on other forensic evidence. The ages of the victims range from 68 to 93 years.

3. Due to the method of attack and fear invoked, many of the witnesses have been unable to provide a good description of their attacker, but all who can have stated that he is a black male, with some additionally indicating that he is a light-skinned black male. Whilst none of the victims have died directly from the attack, a number have died since.

4. The enquiry is led by a Detective Superintendent, supported by a major enquiry team. This enquiry is being conducted with the rigour of a murder enquiry; it is catalogued on HOLMES, the MPS and national major incident IT platform. This system allows the senior investigating officer to identify common links and ensures that data can be shared, if required, with other police forces in the UK. There are 21,500 people of interest who have been suggested following various appeals or from

adopted lines of enquiry. Over 4,500 of these have so far been eliminated, a significant proportion through voluntary DNA sampling.

5. A reward of £40,000 has been authorised for information leading to the arrest of the offender but has so far failed to identify the offender.

6. The most substantial line of enquiry is that provided by the forensic evidence and this paper will focus on the rationale for continuing to develop this line of enquiry. However, many other lines of enquiry continue alongside this work and the nature of that work cannot be discussed in this paper.

7. The UK is one of the leading countries in the use of DNA and advances in the science continue on an almost daily basis. It is clear that the suspect is not recorded on the national DNA database (NDNAD). He may however have a criminal history that pre-dates the general DNA listing in the UK. The National DNA database commenced in 1995. The general running of DNA testing in the UK is overseen by the Custodian within the Home Office with representation on the NDNAD by the Human Genetics Commission.

8. As the suspect in this case is unknown for DNA purposes, additional ground-breaking work has been undertaken by the MPS team supported by a variety of forensic and academic institutions to establish whether the known facts could be used to extrapolate a wider understanding of the offender's background. This work is crucial given the large number of people who have come

to notice in this enquiry and allows the SIO to use this scientific basis to categorise and prioritise those people on an intelligence basis only. Should the suspect be identified an evidential sample would be used to confirm his involvement and form the basis of a prosecution.

9. One particular area of interest and development was ancestral predictions through the DNA crime stain analysis rather than any individuals. The Human Genome project successfully mapped human DNA. A company in Florida has taken this a step further and developed bio-geographical testing based on 177 DNA markers, which have been selected out of the many millions that make up human DNA as showing the most ancestral variance. They test for Asian, Native American, Sub-Saharan and European admixtures. The company have been used in the past by various law enforcement agencies in the USA. This test can help to geographically map individuals whose ancestral background is a mix of those outlined above.

10. This work indicated that this offender's ancestry comprised of an admixture of:

- 82% Sub-Saharan African
- 12% Native American
- 6% European
- 0% Asian

The conclusion for this work is that both of the offenders' parents will originate (ancestrally) from the Caribbean area.

Whilst this work was useful, it still presented a large

geographical area for consideration and merely indicated ancestry, which may be more than one generation removed from the offender.

11. To provide further predictive work based on this modelling, the enquiry team agreed to undertake further controlled sampling from persons with a known ancestral link to the Caribbean. It was crucial that this sample was carefully controlled to ensure that those who purported to meet the criteria could be relied upon for accuracy of information. The enquiry team consulted with the Cultural and Communities Resource Unit and, with the approval of ACPO, the Specialist Crime Directorate undertook to sample volunteers within the MPS. This work was eventually conducted in 2004 with over 50 staff volunteering to provide non-attributable samples. The enquiry team provided specific briefings to the volunteers and other interest groups in the MPS to ensure that the reason for this work was clearly understood. All samples were subsequently destroyed after analysis.

12. The data from this work has helped to narrow the ancestral profile of this offender to one originating from the Windward Islands of the Caribbean. From this work, the enquiry team have been able to re-prioritise many of those coming to notice, to a lower status of interest to the enquiry and, consequently, avoiding questioning of those who are unlikely to be involved.

13. Through the course of the enquiry we have taken legal advice on a number of occasions to ensure that advice remains current and within the law. At present,

there are 21,500 persons of interest within this enquiry. At the very best, one of these is likely to be the offender. The legal advice clarifies the situation and dictates that it would be wrong to arrest all of those individuals. In light of that, officers approach relevant individuals, discuss the case and look for an opportunity to eliminate them from the enquiry. This could be by confirming passport dates showing they were out of the country on the date of a confirmed Minstead attack.

14. If such an opportunity to eliminate does not readily exist, further research is conducted into each individual. Upon explaining the enquiry in general members of the public have been keen to assist. Indeed, this enquiry has been reported widely in the media and results in the public suggesting possible suspects and expressions of outrage. The ultimate means of eliminating anyone is by DNA. If an individual refuses to provide a DNA sample voluntarily, which is their right and has occasionally happened, the Detective Superintendent reviews all the information to establish if the individual can be eliminated by what is already known. Consequently, a documented decision is made as to whether there are reasonable grounds to arrest. Throughout the enquiry, only four individuals have been arrested. To date, over 3,000 DNA samples have been provided voluntarily from individuals that could not be eliminated in any other way. These are only compared against the Minstead crime scene sample; the individual is not placed on the National Database and receives a letter explaining this process.

These samples are retained for the duration of the enquiry to comply with disclosure obligations. Once the suspect is identified, only his sample will be retained and placed on the DNA National Database. All other samples will be destroyed and the individuals notified by letter.

15. On 9 March 2006 MPA members Lord Tope and Bob Neill were fully briefed on Operation Minstead. Lynne Featherstone MP, who had previously been briefed as an MPA member, was also in attendance.

16. The commitment of the MPS to catch this offender remains resolute and we continue to seek new and innovative methods to progress this work. Many other strands of work are also continuing through the use of conventional and covert policing methods. The fact that this offender has not, to our knowledge, offended since 2005 should not allow for any complacency and there are contingency plans in place across the MPS to ensure the early reporting of such offences to ensure the maximum opportunity to capture evidence that will lead to the arrest of this man.

Race and equality impact

1. The work undertaken by the Minstead team has been discussed with community advisors on the boroughs where these offences mainly occur. The Central IAG has also been briefed on the methodology being employed. By taking the approach we have, we continue to ensure that the enquiries are directed proportionately towards solving this series of offences whilst minimising the impact to the

black and elderly communities by focusing on those whose ancestral background meets the criteria from the findings of the latest scientific methods available. This has reduced considerably the number of individuals who may otherwise have been approached from the black communities in connection with this enquiry.

2. The Department of Public Affairs continues to provide media support for this investigation. Community impact is a key consideration when targeting appropriate media and formulating the key messages of any press release. This has included engagement with minority and mainstream media and using internal communication to support and explain the investigation's appeals for staff sampling.

3. Community concerns have been addressed by engaging with a variety of community organisations and public bodies (Bromley elderly community representatives, community meetings, MPs, IPCC etc.). The Black Police Association have also been consulted for guidance and support and are represented on the Gold Group, also composed of representatives from the local communities (where the offender was most active). Following a negative article in *The Voice* newspaper, police released an explanatory article addressing the specific concerns of some of the readers. Briefings have also been provided to Ministers from the three main political parties to support investigative methods and address community concerns. Borough commanders on each of the boroughs where the offences have occurred have also been individually briefed to allow them to provide reassurance to the specific

community groups and CDRP arrangements at a local level. Additionally the SIO continues to make himself available to provide more detailed briefings to interested groups as required.

Financial implications

There are no significant financial implications in relation to this on-going enquiry. Current proposed work is being managed within budget allocations already provided to SCD.'

(NOTE: These are some of the abbreviations used in the report: ACPO Association of Chief Police Officers, CDRP Crime and Disorder Reduction Partnerships, DNA DeoxyriboNucleic Acid, HOLMES Home Office Large Major Enquiry System, IAG Independent Advisory Group, IPCC Independent Police Complaints Commission, IT Information Technology, MPA Metropolitan Police Authority, MPS Metropolitan Police Service, NDNAD National DNA Database, SCD Specialist Crime Directorate, SIO Senior Investigating Officer)

It was a comprehensive assessment of the state of play in the inquiry. By the middle of the next month, October, detectives had flown to the Caribbean to follow up the suggestion that the Night Stalker or his family had originated from there. Mr Morgan said he wished to make clear that, while officers were making an appeal in Trinidad, 'this does not mean that we believe this offender is, in fact, Trinidadian. This criminal operates in south London and has an intricate knowledge of the area. We believe that he resides in the UK but, given his ancestral roots, we believe that he may travel to this region at times, possibly visiting relatives. My appeal is aimed at anyone in the Windward Islands region who believes they may know someone who fits the description and who sometimes comes over for a visit.'

'We need to do whatever we can to stop this man,' Mr Morgan told the *Trinidad Times*, and admitted that, in his 22 years as a police officer, he had never encountered a case like it.

Although there was the case of the woman aged 88 who had been raped twice one night in 1999, suffered a perforated bowel, nearly died during six hours in surgery and lived the rest of her life in agony, Mr Morgan mentioned that, when another victim had told the man that she had an artificial hip, he treated her with less aggression.

The Stalker also would not take cash from a plate by one old woman's front door after she told him it was for her church collection, and would spend as long as four hours in a victim's home, simply because he appeared to enjoy their company.

'Even after going through such an experience, they are not describing him as the nastiest person they have ever met,' Mr Morgan said.

How they responded was a factor in determining what he would do with his victims, he added. Some screamed and he fled. Some asked to use the lavatory and locked themselves in. One chanted the Koran at him until he left. 'What we have noticed is that if a victim challenges him and says, "How dare you? Who do you think you are? What would your mother think of you?" he backs off, behaves like a child, and scurries out and leaves,' Mr Morgan said. 'We have had some very strong characters among the victims – ladies of senior years who have experienced life.'

Of the rest, he said, some were attacked immediately and raped. 'Some he's never attacked and some he walked around the house with and then decided he wanted to have sex.' He may have been seeking domesticity; he might have found the company of older women sexually arousing. He would say little, but a few engaged him in conversation. Sometimes he thanked his victim, kissed them or shook hands. He would say goodbye before he left. It was as if he actually believed they were willing partners, Mr Morgan said.

He usually left by the front door, taking something with him. From one victim he stole two Krugerrands and a half-sovereign; from others a worthless ceramic dish and rosary beads. There had been occasions when he would take credit or debit cards, demand the PIN number and then never even try to use the card. 'Profilers say it's a trophy he wants – something to remind him of the sexual experience he's just enjoyed,' Mr Morgan said.

The Stalker told one victim in 2004 that his mother had died four years earlier, adding 'the government let her down anyway', and also mentioned he needed money to get to Brighton.

In addition, the manner in which he physically handled some of his victims, by supporting their lower spine as they were placed on a sofa or lifting them by their elbows when they arose from a sitting position, gave indications that he had worked with the elderly.

These were the details Mr Morgan's team broadcast in Trinidad, and were to repeat in Barbados, in the hope of a breakthrough.

Mr Morgan felt at that stage that two things had to happen for the Night Stalker to be caught: people had to dismiss their preconceptions and accept that the attacker might be a respected member of the community – someone they could not believe capable of such crimes, and they had to report anybody who might fit the bill, of whatever status, confident that a DNA test would quickly eliminate him if he was innocent.

Mr Morgan had attended the funerals of some victims and admitted to the *Trinidad Times* a degree of emotional involvement in the case, remembering that before she died one woman victim told him, 'The one thing I need to know before I go is who it was and why he did it to me.'

Not all the coverage of the Minstead team's trip to Trinidad was positive. One newspaper, which observed the squad relaxing by the hotel swimming pool or near the bar on the sunny island, referred to them as 'The Frying Squad', although Scotland Yard pointed out: 'Since arriving in Trinidad, the officers have had an intense schedule of appointments, liaised with local law enforcement agencies and put in place arrangements for support for the Operation Minstead.'

One aspect of the Stalker's behaviour being discussed in some quarters was the sexual aspect of his conduct towards his elderly victims and whether he suffered from paraphilia – a condition involving sex fetishes where a person's sexual arousal and gratification depend on fantasising about, and engaging in, sexual behaviour that is atypical and extreme. A paraphilia can revolve around a particular sex fetish such as objects (e.g. children, animals, underwear) or around a particular sex fetish act (e.g. inflicting pain, exposing oneself).

A paraphilia is distinguished by 'a preoccupation with the object or behaviour to the point of being dependent on that object or behaviour for sexual gratification. In most cases, types of sexual activity outside the boundaries of the paraphilia lose their arousal or satisfaction potential unless the person fantasises about the paraphilia at the same time.' Most paraphilias are far more common in men than in women, with the focus usually very specific and unchanging, and the definition seemed to be apt for the Night Stalker and his behaviour towards those old folk.

At the end of November 2006, Operation Minstead was featured once more on *Crimewatch*, this time including an audio tape of a 999 call made by one of the man's victims. Four leading criminal profilers had worked on compiling a picture of the man.

'On a series of occasions he has taken the pulse of his victims,' one detective said. 'They have feigned injury but he has taken their pulse and said, "There's nothing wrong with you." It suggests a skill or expertise which says something about him as an individual. He could be a professional. In all probability he has a family. He could be a medical professional, a care worker; he could work in a home for the elderly. He could have any job which gives him access to the areas where these crimes are committed.'

The programme generated more than 150 calls to the police – without success.

Again, the Night Stalker went quiet, but there was always the fear that he would reappear, and that is exactly what he did just over 18 months later, in May 2008, when he struck at least three times within weeks. He is thought to have sexually assaulted at least two people, bringing his 'official' total number of attacks to 104.

On 12 May, he broke into an elderly woman's home in Norwood. The Night Stalker also carried out an early-hours burglary in Downham near Bromley five days later, and in June the third break-in came at 2am in Lee, also in his south east London stomping ground. Police said the victim was not injured. Each time, telephone wires were cut and light bulbs removed so his features could not be seen through his balaclava.

Police did not reveal full details of the attacks to avoid unnecessarily scaring elderly people in the area, some of whom had taken to sleeping during the day and staying awake at night so they could hear him should he try to break in during the small hours. But one source said, 'He is back and we would urge people to use sensible precautions and be vigilant about their security. The suspect has always struck in clusters and what is happening is very worrying. But it also gives us chances to catch him.'

Scotland Yard also confirmed they were looking at five break-ins at homes in south east London in May and four back in November 2007, all believed to be connected to the man. A total of 108 incidents dating back to 1992 were now being linked to him.

The same month, June 2008, police released an image of a man they believed to be the Night Stalker after one of the man's victims managed to give a description of the attacker. Mr Morgan said, 'Following a recent offence, this artist's impression has been compiled. We are cautious about the offence as it has not been linked forensically, but the manner in which it was committed is consistent with the way the Minstead offender behaves. Despite not having a forensic link, I feel it is important that we release this image. A vulnerable section of society has been terrorised for 18 years and this gives us a real chance of identifying an offender.

'The victim saw the suspect in dark conditions but states he is a light-skinned black man, with markings on the side of his face. These could be a number of things such as freckles, scarring or spots.'

The police thought it was this facial abnormality or distinguishing mark that prompted the Stalker to be doubly sure that his face was as covered as possible during his attacks. It was a theory that was eventually to be justified. 'In the past, victims have been too traumatised to give a detailed description,' Mr Morgan said. 'This witness [one of the victims] is the only one to have seen his face in near-daylight and under a streetlight. What we now know is that he has facial peculiarities that he is extremely concerned about and he knows could lead to his arrest. He has gone to greater extents than normal rapists and burglars to hide the markings.

'What the woman saw is being examined by medical experts who might just be able to pinpoint a distinctive rash or series of spots, maybe growths, that will help identify this man.'

It eventually emerged that he did have a facial characteristic that could have led to his being tracked down earlier: two missing front teeth. He did not wear dentures, so his victims would have been able to give this information to police.

The theory was also aired that the Night Stalker might be a motorcyclist who escaped from his victims' homes on his bike.

In August 2008, the Stalker struck again, this time terrifying an 81-year-old woman in West Wickham but not assaulting or injuring her. In November, there were two more raids within five days of each other. Both the victims were 95 – a woman from West Wickham and a man from Hither Green.

The weeks and months passed and still the police were

no nearer to catching their man. In June 2009, he broke into nine homes in a two-week period and was feared to have carried out a total of 25 attacks so far that year. 'The recent outbreak of incidents would suggest this man is unable to control his compulsions,' said one police source, 'or else he could simply be taunting the police. It has caused deep concern among top brass.'

So great was this concern that, in early November 2009, it emerged that the Metropolitan Police had carried out 2,054 DNA tests at a cost of £102,700 as part of their mammoth inquiry. A team of 29 police officers and staff based at Lewisham police station continued to work to identify him. So much time spent, so many police officers' hours, such a financial cost and an unknown number of traumatised victims going back almost two decades, if not longer. The list seemed endless.

But the Stalker's days were numbered – the breakthrough was just around the corner.

CHAPTER TEN

It ended where it had begun: out in the quiet suburbs where the apple blossom trees flowered in spring but by now had seen their leaves depart for another year. It was suburbia writ large: houses built mainly between the wars along roads whose names contained words like Orchard, Woodlands, Gardens and Freshfields. It was the sort of area where BBC situation-comedies based on lower-middle-class aspirations were set: Hyacinth Bucket territory.

Late that Saturday night, 14 November 2009, it was as quiet a part of Croydon as one could find and the perfect hunting ground for Delroy Grant. This time, however, he was not the one doing the watching.

One of those anonymous houses was unoccupied – empty, that is, except for the two men in the bay-window bedroom on the first floor. They had been there since 10pm and by now it was almost midnight, 11.57pm to be precise. The men were Richard Jenkins and Nathan Coutts, and all they were doing was looking out on to the quiet streets below. There was a reason they were there: they were detectives looking out for the Night Stalker.

The Metropolitan Police Commissioner had made it clear that it was imperative the Stalker be caught. The two men in the empty house were just part of a massive police presence that night out on the streets, in cars and in observation points in the area known to be the Stalker's patch. The obscene mounting tally of victims just had to come to an end sometime. Operation Minstead had 100 men and women out and about that night, and Detective Constable Jenkins and Detective Sergeant Coutts were to be the first to play their part in the capture of Delroy Grant.

They knew that the description of the Stalker was that of a dark-skinned man and that, from previous activity near victims' homes, there was a possibility he might be driving a Vauxhall Zafira. As midnight neared, Det. Con. Jenkins looked out on to the street. 'I saw a black-skinned man running from the direction of number 70,' he said later. The man was wearing a dark top made of shiny material, dark trousers and dark shoes. 'He was running towards me. Initially, when I first saw him, he was about 50 metres away.' It was a dark but clear night and the light was good from the sodium street lighting. The man was getting nearer, about 30 metres by this time. 'From there he went towards a vehicle. I saw the driver's door open.

He got into the driver's door and almost immediately the lights came on.' It was, the officer said, a dark, gun-metal-grey Vauxhall Zafira, the most recent model. 'It picked up speed and it was quickly out of my sight.'

Det. Sgt. Coutts confirmed the sighting and the lighting at that time of night. 'It was perfectly adequate to identify the sex and appearance of an individual,' he said, adding, 'The first time I saw him was when he cleared the tree [that was partly obscuring the officer's view] and he was running.'

Det. Con. Jenkins was on his radio instantly. 'There was more communication on the radio and I heard another officer say that it was travelling at a high speed and then I heard that it had been stopped.'

Other officers had been sitting in unmarked cars in various positions in the area and, when the message of the sighting came over their radios, a posse of them set off to stop the fleeing man in his car.

Det. Con. Michael Keyte was one of them. 'From the position where my car was, I knew I could not catch them [the other cars] up,' he said. Instead, using local knowledge, he headed towards a nearby junction, that of Croydon Road (the A213) and Elmers End Road, which was controlled by traffic lights. There the hunted car was facing him. He could see that it would be turning right, so he turned left. This meant that he was ahead of the Vauxhall once the lights had changed and it had turned right.

'I was travelling slowly at 30mph and he was catching

me up quickly,' the detective continued. 'It then slowed down for speed cameras.' Det. Con. Keyte was acting as a barrier in front of the Vauxhall as other officers, with whom he was in touch, approached the car from behind. They made it stop and Det. Con. Keyte said, 'My car stopped when the Zafira stopped. I was approximately 15 yards ahead. I sat in my car until I could see what was going to happen.'

What was happening was being dictated by the unmarked police vehicle that had been following the suspect's car. In it was Det. Con. David Matthews, who had heard over the radio that a black male had been seen running down the road and leaving in a grey Vauxhall Zafira. 'I saw the vehicle pass and I could see that it had a male driver. He was the only occupant.' Det. Con. Matthews followed as the Zafira overtook a vehicle at a speed in excess of 60mph. 'I had trouble keeping up, to be honest,' the detective admitted.

Other police cars were now heading in its direction as Det. Con. Matthews followed the Vauxhall on its journey past the King Edward pub and South Norwood Country Park. The Zafira was travelling at high speed but it slowed down for the 'Gatso', the roadside speed camera. 'I was asked by my sergeant [over the radio] that when I felt happy I should stop the vehicle.' It was a narrow stretch of road so he put on his siren and blue flashing light and the Vauxhall pulled over. 'I was anticipating that, if this was the man, he would run so I drew alongside him.'

He approached the driver, the window was down and the door was locked. 'He was quite calm and very quiet and I noticed that his trousers were unbuttoned and partially opened at the front. I identified myself and took the keys out of the vehicle.

'I have been in the police years for more than 20 years and normally when you stop someone, certainly late at night, they will ask you, "Why have you stopped me?" or they will say something. He said nothing.'

It was approximately 15 minutes past midnight on the Sunday morning by this time and as the detective took charge of the keys and his colleagues converged on the scene in Witham Road, Beckenham, Delroy Grant must have known his time was up. The two decades of chaos and fear he had brought to south London and beyond was over.

Initially, the driver said his name was 'Kelvin Grant' but then a credit card was discovered in the vehicle with 'D Grant' on it. Asked his name again, he said, 'Delroy Easton,' and then later said, 'Delroy Grant.'

He was handcuffed and police noticed a bulge in his left front pocket. One of the other officers on the scene, Det. Con. Andrew Stone, took a small torch out of the driver's pocket. Grant was to say later that the torch had been planted on him by the officers, accusations they both strongly denied.

More police arrived on the scene and in the Vauxhall they found a black woolly hat in the glove compartment and also a pair of bolt cutters, crowbar and pliers. There was £97.12 in cash on Grant too. Asked what he did for a living, he said he was 'a carer' and when asked what he was doing out that night said he had been 'waiting outside the Co-op to buy some puff [marijuana] but the guy had not turned up'. The officers at the scene called for a police van and 15 minutes later it arrived.

Grant was taken to Lewisham police station – his car went to the police car pound in Croydon – where he was presented to the custody sergeant, the officer responsible for the care of those arrested. On this occasion, it was a Sgt. Ritchie.

Then Grant was taken to a private room, where he was told to take off his clothes, to be presented with alternative clothing. As he did so, police saw that he had on two pairs of jeans – one black and one dark denim, and three shirts – one black short-sleeve shirt, one brown long-sleeve shirt and a white short-sleeved shirt with a print of 'Barclays Bank' and a cartoon bird on it. He was also wearing two pairs of underpants and had a sock through the loop on the waistband of his trousers.

He was arrested and cautioned but made no reply. Two DNA swabs were now taken from him, which were to be sent to the Forensic Service at Lambeth. Grant's clothes were taken in a bag and presented to the custody sergeant, who made a note of them as part of the routine used when a person is taken into custody.

At 5.15am, Grant was interviewed by Det. Sgt. Adam Spier and a colleague. They cautioned him and asked if he had visited any vulnerable people that night. They were worried that, if he had struck as the Night Stalker, there might still be an elderly person in distress somewhere who was in need of help and attention. He replied, 'I have not visited anyone.'

Later, he was questioned again and told he should ask if there was anything he did not understand. His response was to say, 'Due to the serious allegations I would like to say "no comment" to the questions you are going to ask me. I am still in a state of shock.'

He still refused to comment when, during the day at different times, he was questioned about the clothes found in his car, the tools that were discovered, and the DNA samples taken at previous crime scenes which matched his. He replied 'No comment' to them all, apart from saying he knew who the jacket in his car belonged to, but he would not name the owner.

At one stage, his fingerprints were taken and he remarked to the officer performing the task, 'I don't know why you are bothering – I always wear gloves.' It was a remark that he was subsequently to deny and was to feature in his trial. It was one, he later said, that was made in jest. What he had actually said, in a light-hearted manner, was that, 'if' he had carried out the crimes, then he would have worn gloves to do so, he was to claim. The next day at Grant's home in Brockley Mews, Brockley, police found a homemade eye mask, two or three torches, a pair of size 10 Adidas trainers and various screwdrivers and chisels.

By now, the news was out – the police were almost

certain they'd captured the Night Stalker. A Scotland Yard spokesman said, 'We can confirm a 52-year-old man was arrested in the early hours of Sunday morning in a pre-planned operation. He is currently in custody at a London police station.'

The Press Association, the national news agency relied on by newspapers, television and radio for much of their news, reported that evening:

'Detectives were tonight waiting to learn if they have finally caught the most prolific rapist-burglar to stalk Britain's streets. They have been hunting the attacker, dubbed the "Night Stalker", since a pattern of crimes first emerged in the early 1990s. Investigators have recovered at least 10 DNA samples from victims, many of them elderly, who were targeted in their homes across south London. It should take just hours for forensic scientists to confirm if the 52-year-old suspect in their custody is the man who has eluded them for so long.

'The arrest, at an unknown location in the capital, came after rumours emerged last week that senior officers believed they were close to nailing the case. It is not known if someone will finally claim the £40,000 reward for information about his identity after tipping off detectives. One source close to the inquiry said the arrest was "significant" and investigators are extremely excited. More than 17 years after his first offence, some 30 officers and staff at Lewisham police station continued to work to identify the culprit as part of Operation Minstead. The inquiry team amassed a remarkable body of evidence. The Met said tonight there had been previous arrests, but a spokesman could not confirm exactly how many.

'The light-skinned black man targeted elderly people and is responsible for more than 100 offences in the south London area dating back to 1990. The criminal has a distinctive pattern of behaviour, often disabling telephone lines and fuse boxes before breaking into the homes of vulnerable people. Light bulbs have also been removed and curtains drawn. In some cases the tools used to gain entry, sometimes by removing entire double glazed units, have been taken from the victim's shed.'

The report went on to say: 'The total number of raids linked to the man during his 19-year reign of terror was understood to be at least 108. The attacks have taken place in clusters in south and south east London, including Dulwich, Orpington, Norwood, Downham, Lee, West Wickham and Bickley. The most recent linked burglaries took place in June, when one of nine break-ins was linked to the suspect by DNA. Two of the burglaries took place in Shirley, Croydon. The culprit is thought to be an employed black man, aged between 35 and 45, who masks his crimes behind the veneer of a respectable life. He is believed to be a gerontophile, someone with a sexual fixation with the elderly. Police said the man has raped four people and sexually assaulted 24 others.'

On Monday, 16 November, Grant appeared at Greenwich Magistrates' Court charged with five rapes, six indecent assaults and eleven burglaries between 1992 and 2009. He appeared in the dock wearing a white, police-issue, long-sleeved tracksuit, flanked by two women custody officers, and spoke only to confirm his personal details, giving his middle name as Easton.

Prosecutor Denise Clewes asked for Grant to be remanded back into police custody until the following Thursday as enquiries were continuing. She said, 'This is a case where the usual reporting restrictions do apply. I ask for three days laid down in police custody. Police wish to speak to Grant about a large number of other offences. Further charges are likely. There is still evidence that needs to be gathered and officers have not had the time to do this.'

Janet Lloyd, representing Grant, made no application for bail.

There was a short adjournment during the 20-minute hearing so a point of law could be checked. District Judge Angus Hamilton then remanded Grant in police custody and ordered him to appear at the same court later in the week.

The charges at that stage were:

12 October 1992 Raping an 89-year-old woman in Shirley, Croydon.

5 September 1998 Raping an 81-year-old woman in Warlingham, Surrey.

20 June 1999 Burglary with violence at a home in Beckenham, south east London.

28 July 1999 Raping an 82-year-old woman in Addiscombe, near Croydon.

5 August 1999 Raping an 88-year-old woman in Orpington, Kent.

20 June 1999 Indecently assaulting a 71-year-old woman in Beckenham, south east London.

7 December 1999 Indecently assaulting an 82-year-old woman in Addiscombe, near Croydon.

4 August 1999 Indecently assaulting an 88-year-old woman in Shirley, near Croydon.

13 October 2002 Indecently assaulting a 77-year-old woman in Shirley, near Croydon.

25 May 2009 Burglary at a home in Shortlands, Bromley.

12 October 1992 Burglary with violence at a home in Shirley, near Croydon.

5 September 1998 (two charges) Burglary with intent to rape at a home in Warlingham, Surrey. Indecently assaulting an 81-year-old woman.

12 July 1999 Burglary with violence at a home in Addiscombe, near Croydon.

28 July 1999 (two charges) Burglary with violence at a home in Addiscombe, near Croydon. Indecently assaulting an 82-year-old woman.

4 August 1999 Burglary with violence at a home in Shirley, near Croydon.

5 August 1999 (two counts) Burglary with violence at a home in Orpington, Kent. Raping an 88-year-old woman.

13 October 2002 Burglary with violence at a home in Shirley, near Croydon.

7 March 2003 Burglary with violence at a home in West Dulwich, south London.

7 September 2004 Burglary with violence at a home in Bromley, south east London.

Even as Grant stood in the dock, forensic officers were conducting their search of his three-storey end-of-terrace home in Brockley Mews, sandwiched between Honor Oak Crematorium and a busy railway line. The police had descended on the house and cordoned it off. In the garden of the property, weight-lifting equipment, a punch bag and children's toys could be seen as the officers, clad all in white, carried out their work. The media, too, had arrived in force.

One neighbour, 58, was the first to reveal that Grant's wife Jennifer had been struck down by multiple sclerosis and was confined to a wheelchair. The neighbour said the couple, both dedicated Jehovah's Witnesses, had lived there for about 19 years and had four children – two girls in their twenties and at university and two grown-up boys.

He said of Grant, 'He was quiet but if you knew him he would talk to you. After his wife had the youngest boy she just went down. She got MS. He was her full-time carer. He looked after her night and day. He had converted the garage into a bedroom for her.

'He would go for a drink at some of the pubs around here and played dominoes at the Royal British Legion. He would go once a month. He was a genuinely nice person.

He used to go out late at night and I thought he was a cab driver. He has also done a bit of painting and decorating.'

He added that Grant would come with his wife and sons for community barbecues and he always helped with the cooking. 'He was brilliant. He was a genuinely nice person.'

Another neighbour said he had known Grant for 17 years. 'He was a good friend of mine. We cooked together, drank together, ate together – it is hard to believe. He was a calm and cool character. He took care of his wife and we respected him for that. I don't know exactly where he was from. It may have been Tobago, some small island in the Caribbean.

'If we held a barbecue in the street, he would push his wife down and we would all enjoy ourselves. Before his wife got sick, he used to be a chippy – a carpenter. He fitted kitchens and things like that. He was dressed nice at all times – not a ragamuffin.'

Outside the garage that Grant had converted into a bedroom for his wife was a rudimentary punch bag, which locals said was filled with cement. On the decking was a set of weights and a radio-controlled car, and there was a dartboard hanging on the back wall. On the trees overhanging the garden were several plastic bottles, riddled with holes. Nearby residents said that Grant owned an air rifle and used the bottles for target practice. 'He asked me to get him some proper targets,' one said. 'I've got them in my house, but I didn't get the chance to give them to him.'

Other neighbours confirmed the locals' impression of Grant as a well-thought-of man and that his arrest had come as a 'complete shock'. One said, 'He always looked smart and respectable and was completely devoted to his wife and children. He was a pretty normal bloke. He would talk about fishing. There was a part of him that was very shy and he was devoted to his wife. His kids were the politest and nicest round here. I just can't believe it could be him. In the summer months we would have barbecues and he would bring his people carrier down and turn the stereo on. Everyone thought he was a great bloke.'

The same resident added, 'I used to see him going out late at night and coming back at three or four in the morning. I thought he was working as a cabbie. Sometimes in the summer I might be still sat with my balcony open and he would give me a beep.'

Across the footbridge that spanned the railway line near his home was a house where Grant's wife used to meet fellow Jehovah's Witnesses. Women there said that Jennifer Grant had been a member of the religion for about 20 years, before her illness. They added that at first Grant would attend the house, or the nearby Forest Hill Kingdom Hall on David's Road, only to drop off or collect his wife, but later he became a Jehovah's Witness too.

Because of her illness, the pair stopped attending the Kingdom Hall and became 'disassociated' – the term members use for Witnesses who lapse. Jennifer Grant was later persuaded to return, but her husband did not join her. One fellow member who knew the couple said, 'He got involved and came to a few meetings, but he was never very enthusiastic. She was very tall, slim and glamorous until her illness struck. After her illness she lost the use of her legs. She used to tell everyone, "Look after your legs."'

Harley Burford, a minister at the Kingdom Hall where the Grants worshipped, described them as a warm and close couple. 'Everyone in the congregation will be shocked by the news. They seemed very close and very warm and were a lovely family. Our thoughts and prayers are with Jennifer and her family and of course with all the victims.'

Grant's friends and neighbours weren't the only ones taken aback by his arrest. His first wife Janet, who was to be a key witness in his trial 18 months later, was also stunned by the news. But her remarks were indicative of the true character of Delroy Grant. According to her, he went berserk if there was a 'speck of dust' in their house – and even lost control of his temper as she was about to have their second boy. Janet, 53, said, 'I was hours away from giving birth and he didn't care.'

Janet, who divorced Grant after a three-year marriage, added, 'He was very charming and sophisticated. I thought I'd found my soulmate. But then the violence started. Within weeks, he showed his real character. He flew at me over our house being a mess. There was no warning – it just came. He was what you would call a clean freak. He was obsessed about dirt. Everything didn't just have to be tidy – it had to be set straight, laid out and spotless. Once, he lifted up our bed to inspect the dust underneath and went mad when he found a speck or two. He shouted and screamed before calming down again. He wasn't sexually violent but if things weren't clean he'd fly into a rage. He was obsessive about it. After his temper had subsided, he went back to being the same charming guy he'd been before, as if nothing had happened.

'Looking back now, it was a horrible time for me. I lived with it for years. I'd locked that part of my life away. But when Delroy was arrested on Sunday it all came flooding back.'

Janet, a carer who married Grant after a whirlwind romance, said, 'I'd watch *Crimewatch* on TV. I knew all about the Night Stalker. I work with elderly people and to see that going on was frightening. It was happening in areas near where I lived. If I'd been given even an inkling, I would have been the first to pick up the phone and call the police.'

She said Grant barely had any contact with their sons. 'If Delroy has done these crimes, he will be revelling in all the attention. He always was a vain pretty boy and loved to think he was the centre of everyone's eye. The idea of him being in the newspapers and on TV will make him happy, even if it's for all the wrong reasons.'

She added, 'I'd often catch him with other women. He would attack me for confronting him about it. He had this idea he could get away with it because he was too clever. But he wasn't clever enough for me.'

Delroy Junior, 35 said, 'We never clicked with him.'

His brother Michael, 32, added, 'Our dad wasn't a father.'

Grant went on to have three more sons with second wife Jennifer, including Jason and Louis.

Metropolitan Police Commissioner Sir Paul Stephenson's determination to catch the Night Stalker had played a major part in his capture. A source close to the Commissioner was quoted as saying: 'This is one of the greatest days for the Metropolitan Police. Millions of man hours have gone into this. To get a breakthrough like this takes your breath away. The best bit is it didn't come from a tip-off or DNA screening but from old-fashioned detective work. It makes you proud to be a cop.'

Unfortunately, that euphoria was somewhat short-lived. One of the first things that detectives did once Grant had been arrested was to check the Operation Minstead details and they realised that his name had cropped up before. He had slipped through their net. We will look at this in detail later, but the weekend after Grant's arrest it emerged that years earlier there had been two chances to catch the Stalker.

Grant had first come to police attention in 1999 when a house was burgled in Orpington. Details of the break-in – telephone wires were cut and the house plunged into darkness – matched the classic methods of the Night Stalker. A sharp-eyed member of the local neighbourhood watch team, having seen a man get out of a car and act suspiciously in his street, took down the car's registration number and immediately reported it to police. That vital information identified Grant as a suspect. Tragically, officers followed up the information by knocking on the door of the wrong Delroy Grant, whose DNA was taken and not surprisingly it eliminated him from the inquiry.

That blunder led directly to the second occasion when Grant was allowed to escape, after an e-fit of the serial rapist being hunted had been issued by the police. A caller rang Crimestoppers to tell them he thought he recognised the man as Delroy Grant. Officers were asked to follow it up but when they checked police records, found that 'Delroy Grant' had been eliminated from the inquiry and so never questioned the man the caller had actually identified.

A police source said, 'There is a course of events that went on in 1999 that are being looked at. When you involve humans, it will always be open to error. With an investigation that has gone on for as long as this, there was always going to be criticism. It would be very odd to suggest over the course of a 17-year investigation there were not lessons to be learned.'

It also became obvious that many of the cases against Grant would involve the testimonies of elderly people who had died since the night that the Stalker came to visit them. They had given detailed statements – including some recorded on video – about their ordeals to detectives from Operation Minstead and those tapes were likely to form a crucial part of the prosecution case when Grant went on trial.

Fearing other victims would be unable to give evidence

because of their age, officers checked and rechecked their statements. One officer said, 'The team wanted to make sure the testimony was preserved as best as possible for future use, even if the victims were not around to be examined on it. They have always been mindful the victims were elderly, not always in good health and had also suffered terrible shocks. They've been planning for this moment for years.'

Grant appeared in court as arranged on the Thursday after his arrest and again the following week. Both times, he was remanded in custody and in February 2010 he appeared at Maidstone Crown Court via a video link, when he was remanded again. In June that year, he made his first appearance at The Old Bailey, where he appeared in the dock dressed smartly in a pin-striped suit and wearing a light-blue tie, and flanked by three security guards. The court was crowded for this first appearance, with some relatives of his alleged victims sitting in the public gallery.

As the indictment was read to him, beginning with a burglary in Shirley, south London, in October 1992 and comprising three rapes, an attempted rape, six indecent assaults, a sexual assault, 16 burglaries and two attempted burglaries, Grant replied 'not guilty' to each count. It took 15 minutes for him to plead not guilty to all the charges.

It was decided that his trial would take place at Woolwich Crown Court in March 2011 – and what a dramatic trial it was to be.

CHAPTER ELEVEN

Woolwich Crown Court is not the foreboding Victorian building so typical of many major courts in Britain. It is a modern, soulless construction, one of the dozen or so Crown courts serving the London area. It stands in an almost forgotten hinterland of south east London, alongside a busy dual carriageway that has to be negotiated to reach the unprepossessing group of shops opposite: a Tesco Express, a cashpoint, a drop-in health centre and a pub which in March 2011 boasted a weekday carvery at £3.99 per head (payable in advance). Parents from the nearby estate bring their toddlers in to play in front of the giant television screen as they devour their beef, turkey or gammon, complete with Yorkshire puddings and dry balls of sage and onion stuffing.

Alongside the Crown court is Belmarsh Prison. Because prisoners can be brought to court via an underground tunnel, Woolwich has become a favoured venue for high-security trials. Delroy Grant had been in custody at Belmarsh, so his journey to court every day would be a short one. And it was in court number three at Woolwich, in front of Judge Peter Rook QC, that his sensational trial began on 3 March.

This was not just the first time that the world at large had heard a chronological narrative of the Stalker's crimes. It was the first time that Grant's amazing defence – to be presented over the following three weeks – became public. His explanation of how his DNA came to be discovered at the scenes of the crimes and his accusations towards members of his family were astonishing.

Wearing a pin-striped suit and flanked by three prison guards in short-sleeved white shirts (one woman and two men), Grant denied all the charges against him. He was impassive at the start of the trial, as he was for most of the proceedings, occasionally putting on spectacles to look at documents he had alongside him, or nodding slightly when he concurred or shaking his head to express disagreement.

Two days had already been spent in legal argument before the jury of seven men and five women heard the dramatic opening of the case by Jonathan Laidlaw QC, prosecuting. Described shortly before the case began by the *Sunday Times* as 'the country's leading prosecutor', Mr Laidlaw displayed an easily understandable rhythm of delivery and crystal-clear voice as he spelled out for the jury the Crown's case against Grant.

The case he outlined – transmitted via television, radio and news agency reports around the world – merits repeating in detail. (The only amendments made here to his opening speech are the removal of any clues to the victims' identities – these have been replaced with letters: A, B, C, etc. – or references to exhibits and their numbering which, although understandable to the jury members, would be confusing to the reader who cannot see them. It is also important to remember that Mr Laidlaw was addressing only the charges that Grant faced at his trial, not the many other offences he may have been linked with.)

Mr Laidlaw told the jury, 'The defendant, as you have heard, is charged with 29 offences committed over the course of 17 years between October 1992 and November 2009. The offences relate to 18 separate incidents, so 18 occasions during that period when the defendant committed burglaries in the south London area. His offences, the burglaries he committed were not, however, of the usual sort: the sort of offending which is upsetting enough and which will inconvenience each of us at some point or other in our lives.

'The defendant's offending was of an altogether different sort and was of a far, far more serious and sinister nature because, in what was to become something of a campaign, the defendant was targeting the elderly and the vulnerable in their homes and during the night. This is why he was to become known as the "Night Stalker". Most of his victims were in their eighties: the eldest being 89 years old. Neither, I am afraid and as the nature of the additional charges discloses, was his criminality confined or defined only by a financial motive. He was not just breaking into their homes in order only to steal and to make money.

'There was also a sexual element to his offending, because on four of the occasions he committed burglaries the defendant went on also to rape or to attempt to rape his elderly female victims. Neither was it just rapes that he indulged in: others amongst his elderly victims were subjected to the most serious of indecent assaults. The nature of his sexual acts he committed seems, in part to have been determined by the reaction of the individual victim. Those who were too frightened to resist or protest were attacked. Where he experienced resistance and where his elderly victims refused to be compliant, they tended to be left alone.

'What it was that motivated him to carry out sexual offences on the very elderly, and what sort of gratification he could possibly have achieved, is obviously difficult if not impossible to understand. Neither was his sexual interest confined only to women, although it was single women living on their own upon which he was focused. Two of the offences with which you are concerned were committed at the homes of old men and they were both subjected to humiliating and degrading sexual assaults. Whether it was just the additional sexual element that he enjoyed or it was the power and control he could assert whilst committing these offences or it was the fear and anxiety, which he created and revelled in, will probably remain unclear.

'Let me, at this early stage of my introduction to the case, and before I come to tell you how it was that the police were eventually to arrest him and then the issues in the case you will be required to resolve, set out for you something of the nature of the offences the prosecution suggest he was responsible for, how he committed those offences and his particular method of offending.

'The first of the attacks that figure in the indictment was a burglary and rape committed at a bungalow in Shirley occupied by an old lady, then 89 years old. Like each of the burglaries, it was carried out late at night and like all but one of the other incidents, the victim was living alone at the address that the defendant had selected for entry. On 11 October 1992, she went to bed but later that night she was woken by the defendant who had appeared, standing over her, masked and gloved in her bedroom. He had broken in by way of a kitchen window. In the bedroom, the defendant asked for money and then took time to search the room before turning his attention to the old woman and to raping her.

'When he had gone, the police were to discover something of the defendant's careful preparation for carrying out his attacks. He had removed light bulbs from the bedroom, no doubt to make any identification of him the more difficult, and he had cut the telephone line at the address, so he would have more time to make good his escape. This would become something of a hallmark to his offending and is a feature of a number of the other burglaries carried out by him. But despite these precautions the defendant did not rush and was not normally in any sort of hurry to leave. He was comfortable in the homes of those he burgled and he often engaged his elderly victims in conversation.

'Six years later, in 1998, the offender would attempt to rape again. This time his victim was 81, immobile and almost housebound. Despite it being absolutely clear that his victim was too old to have penetrative sex he still tried to rape her. His victim would die of unrelated causes the next year, so she was to suffer this attack in the last year of her life. During the summer of 1999, the defendant was to commit six further burglaries and there was also an attempted burglary. On the occasions he was successful in gaining entry to his victims' homes, he indecently assaulted three of the victims and raped two old ladies, one aged 82, the other 88 years old.

'The rapes in 1999 were to be the last rapes committed by him, although he was not, as you will hear, to entirely abandon the sexual element to his offending. Why he should stop carrying out rapes in 1999 is not clear, although it may, in part, have had something to do with the advances in forensic science. Not only was the use of DNA becoming better understood by the criminal fraternity, but also the ability of the scientists to produce results from very small amounts of body fluid recovered at crime scenes was advancing. It was also in 1999 that the media appeal for help in tracing the offender was stepped up. Perhaps, in part, that also persuaded the defendant to begin to abandon his attempts to rape.

'The next burglary in this series of offences with which the defendant is charged was committed at the home of a 77-year-old woman in October 2002. Although he attacked her and tried to force her legs apart as if he were about to rape her, she persuaded him not to do so. There was another burglary in 2003 during which the defendant was to wash the elderly victim's hand in an obvious attempt to remove any of his DNA, and during the later stages of his offending he was to display a greater regard to the importance from his perspective of being careful, of not leaving clues as to his identity.

'Then, in 2004, the defendant was to commit another burglary of the sort I have described. On this occasion, his 84-year-old victim awoke to find the defendant's gloved hand over her mouth and he stole money from the address.

'There is then, in the offences with which the defendant is charged, a five-year gap before the last series of burglaries committed by the defendant begins, which were to end with his arrest in November 2009. This cluster of offences that involved him committing six offences of burglary or attempted burglary began in May 2009 and his method of operating was much the same as before. He almost always gained entry by way of forcing or sometimes removing windows to the rear of the targeted premises. Once inside, he kept the lights out and displayed a disarming degree of confidence as he took his time to search for property to steal. Only one of these victims, an 88-year-old man, was subjected to a sexual attack, but the defendant's treatment of this old man was particularly humiliating.

'Finally, during the night of 14/15 November 2009, the defendant's luck was to depart him. That night he was in Shirley and about to burgle the home of an 86-year-old woman. She was housebound and in a wheelchair, so she would have been another easy victim. But at the address and before he could gain entry, he was disturbed and he made off, running back to his car which was parked nearby. Police officers on covert surveillance duties – part of the long-running Operation Minstead team investigating the activities of the so-called "Night Stalker" – were in the area and watched as the defendant left the scene at speed. Some distance away, in Croydon, the defendant was arrested. The police had their breakthrough and the defendant's offending was finally to be brought to an end.

'The difficulties confronting the police in their efforts to detect and catch an intruder carrying out offences of this sort will immediately be obvious to you. He was committing his offences at night and he was invariably masked, so any subsequent visual identification of him would be almost impossible. In respect of those he raped or subjected to sexual attacks, the defendant, no doubt, was working on the basis that it would be difficult enough for any victim of a sexual offence committed during the trauma of an attack carried out in their own homes and at night to provide reliable descriptions. For the elderly, the position was likely to be even more difficult. In addition to the terrifying nature of the offending, there would be the inevitable confusion and every chance that those he attacked might suffer from dementia or Alzheimer's. There was a good chance they might not even be capable of reporting what had happened.

'From the very beginning and at the outset of his offending, as will be clear to you already, the defendant was conscious of the importance, from his perspective, of leaving as few clues as to his identity at the scenes of his crimes as was possible. Gloves were worn so that he would not leave fingerprints. Back in 1992, DNA identification from recovered body fluids as an investigative tool was in its infancy, and so certainly in the early offences in this sequence the defendant would have had no reason to fear from having left his semen or saliva. There would, of course, be none of his blood. If he was careful, the police would have to get lucky or he would have to be careless. Later, in 1999, there was that change in the pattern of his offending I have spoken of. Did that, in part, coincide with his appreciation that leaving semen at the scenes was no longer a matter of little concern and he would, from that point on, need to exercise a little more restraint if he was to continue to evade arrest?

'The attacks were also, as again you will immediately understand, obviously the result of very careful preparation and planning. It was not by chance that he only carried out offences at the homes of the elderly and those living alone. He must have taken time to conduct reconnaissance in order to identify his targets. He was also well equipped. There were the tools that he used to force windows or to remove them and, as you will hear, he had changes of clothing available to him.

'To the evidence, which links him to this catalogue of offences: it falls, broadly speaking, into three different categories. Firstly, DNA evidence. With the advances in DNA techniques, the scientists were able to go back to the samples taken from the victims and, years later, they were able to recover DNA not only from the semen left by the defendant in the course of the rapes, but also in his saliva following some of the other sexual attacks and burglaries that he committed. Let me make this clear: this was not sampling done at the time. In 1992, DNA was not routinely collected from semen but with the advances in this particular investigative technique, the scientists were able to return to old samples and to carry out fresh testing many years on. Following his arrest, a sample of the defendant's DNA was obtained and his DNA and his profile matches that of the DNA recovered at 12 of the 18 incidents. The scientists, as you will hear, use a figure called the "match probability" figure to express the chances of finding the same profile in an unrelated member of the population. Most of the match probability figures in this case are one in one billion.

'Next, during the cluster of 1999 offences, the defendant was using a particular tool, something like a screwdriver, to gain entry and it is this thing, and the unique tooling marks left by it, which establish he was also responsible for two further burglaries during this period. As for the final four burglaries, the evidential links are by way of the vehicle the defendant was then using and property recovered in it. CCTV links the car and the defendant to the use of cards stolen during these burglaries, and clothing and a crowbar recovered in the car provides further evidence of the defendant's guilt.

'So what is the defendant's defence to these charges? What is he going to say to you, his jury? How is he going to attempt to explain, by way of example and just focusing on the scientific evidence, how his DNA came to be found in the swabs taken by doctors from the victims he raped and elsewhere at the addresses he burgled? Faced with such an apparently strong, if not an overwhelming case, with his DNA being at 12 of the 18 scenes of these crimes, etc., what can he say?

'Well, when the police following his arrest interviewed him, he said nothing at all and he provided not a hint of any genuine defence. All he was to do was to make no comment to the questions asked of him. He obviously needed time to think. Time, unless he was to accept the inevitable, to come up with something which might provide him with a defence. There was just a hint of what was to come, and of his stubborn refusal to face up to the obvious, in an incident that occurred whilst he was still in police custody.

'On 19 November 2009, he was seen in his cell. The

police were doing no more than providing him with deodorant and had no intention of interviewing him. But during that visit the defendant suggested that the police should consider looking at his son as a candidate for this catalogue of offending. He was apparently desperate enough to have suggested that his own son may be responsible, arriving at him as an alternative candidate presumably because he hoped that his son might share his DNA profile. His son does not have the same profile. It is a quite different one and so that as a defence, if the defendant was contemplating running that one, was not going to work.

'So what is the defendant going to say to you, in the hope of introducing some doubt and of persuading you that he may not be guilty of these charges? Well, fairly recently, in a written document provided in January of this year, the defendant has set out the defence he has decided to run.

'Let me introduce you to this. First, he denies having committed any of these offences: so not a single burglary and certainly not any of the sexual attacks. Instead, the defendant is going to say that it is he who has also been a victim in this case in a quite extraordinary attempt by his ex-wife to frame him. This is what he has come up with. He is going to say that his ex-wife, a lady called Mrs Janet Watson, collected and saved samples of his body fluids – so both semen and saliva – during their relationship and then, motivated by malice and in order to satisfy a grudge that she holds against him, she has set about this plot to implicate him. How she would know back in 1979 that in due course the scientists – who had not even then invented the technique – would be able to recover DNA from semen and saliva is a question you might well ask.

'It could not, of course, have been Mrs Watson who carried out the burglaries and the rapes and the other sexual attacks: a male undoubtedly committed these. So the elaborate plot involves Mrs Watson using another man to commit the offences, and, so the defendant will say, using a syringe to leave the defendant's semen and saliva at the scenes of these attacks.

'It is, as I say, a quite extraordinary claim and, I am sorry to say, it is a further indication of what little regard this defendant has for his victims and what he has done.

'There are also some rather obvious problems with this defence, which you will no doubt consider in due course. First, however badly the defendant and his ex-wife had got on and however appallingly he may have treated her during their marriage, do you think for one moment she would fix on a scheme such as this? Or is it clear to you that it is the defendant who has dreamed this story up for the purposes of this trial?

'Next, the timings are rather inconvenient for the defendant. His relationship with Mrs Watson came to an end in 1979. The first offence in the series with which the defendant is charged was not committed until 1992. Is it to be suggested that she bided her time for 13 years – carefully storing his body fluids during this period – before persuading a male associate to begin committing these burglaries and rapes, at which he left samples of the defendant's semen as part of her scheme to get back at the defendant?

'Perhaps more to the point, no victim, in any of their accounts of what happened, makes any mention of seeing the intruder with a syringe or anything like that, and the scientists found no trace of this individual, so no third-party DNA from another male person was recovered. If there was another man raping these old ladies, why was there not a second DNA profile recovered, by way of example, from the vaginal swabs? Was this unknown man able to carry out all these offences without leaving any of his semen, saliva, etc.?

'Finally, how does the "plot by the ex-wife" account explain away, in the last in this series of offences when the links are not DNA links, the connection to the car the defendant was driving and the clothing and articles found in it?

'It is, and I make no apology for saying this again, an extraordinary defence for the defendant to run, borne perhaps in part by the arrogance which characterises his offending and which makes him incapable of facing up to what he has done. But, that said, it is always a defendant's right to require a jury to return verdicts upon him and you will have to give it careful and serious attention. These are very grave charges that he faces, so you will have to examine the accounts of the victims – all of which will be read or played to you – [and] the evidence against the defendant, to see if there is any possibility of anyone else having carried out the offences.

'Having introduced you in general terms to the nature of the allegations made by the prosecution and to the defendant's case, let me now turn to the evidence in a little more detail.

'Counts 1 and 2: the burglary in Shirley and the rape of Miss A during the night of 11/12 October 1992.

'The first of the attacks in the sequence with which the defendant is charged was to occur during the night of Sunday, 11 October 1992, when the defendant was to burgle [the home in Shirley] and to rape the occupier. ... A's sister died in August 1992, so shortly before the burglary, and from that point the victim lived alone at the address. She was then 89 years old: she died in 2005.

'At about 21.15 on the Sunday night of the attack, Miss A felt tired and she prepared for bed. She washed, and then put on her pyjamas and she got into bed at about 21.45 where she read. Miss A heard a slight knocking sound at about this time but thought no more of it: she was living next to a main road and sounds like that were not unusual. The victim could not sleep immediately so, at about 22.30, she made herself a cup of coffee, before going back to bed shortly after 22.30 where she began to read again.

'A few minutes later, Miss A noticed that the door to her bedroom was being opened slowly and a man appeared in the doorway. Entry had been gained to the address by a kitchen window to the rear of the premises. She said, "What are you doing here?" and he moved quickly to her, covering her mouth with a gloved hand. Her attacker – this defendant as the forensic evidence many years later was to establish – was dressed in a grey pullover, a dark jacket and dark trousers and he was wearing a balaclava. He shouted at her to be quiet. Miss A asked, '"What do you want – money?" and she got out of bed and gave the defendant what she had in her purse, £25 in cash. The defendant then said, "They told me that you had a lot of money." In fact, Miss A had a safe, the key to which she had hidden between the mattresses on her bed.

'The defendant then looked out of the window, presumably to check that the coast was clear, before removing the bulbs from the light in both the bedroom and the hallway. Having walked around the bedroom, picking up and looking at letters and papers, he turned his attention to the victim who by this point was sitting on the edge of the bed.

'He bent down, put his hands to her face so as to hold it still and then pressed his mouth to Miss A's in an attempt to kiss her. She shouted out, "Stop it please, you're hurting me!" but he continued to press his lips to hers and then he tried to force his tongue into the old lady's mouth. Next, the defendant forced the victim's legs apart and, pressing down on her, he then raped her. He continued to hold Miss A's face, pressing so hard that her false teeth were dislodged. As she was raped, Miss A cried out, telling him that he was hurting her.

'Having searched the room and found the keys to the

safe, the defendant took a brown wallet containing £250 and some jewellery. Using a torch, he looked into the other rooms before leaving the address by the back door. Miss A picked up the telephone to call her niece who lived close by, but the line was dead: the defendant had disconnected the line before the rape.

'Miss A's description of her assailant and her ability to identify him is important and illustrative of the point I made a little earlier. This defendant was well prepared. He wore a mask and he knew there was little chance that his elderly victims would be able to identify him. Miss A was able to provide only this description of him: her assailant was about 6 feet [tall], 22 years old, black with brown eyes. She could provide no other description of his face because of the balaclava and she said she would not be able to identify him again.

'Being unable to telephone for help or to call the police, Miss A dressed and went on foot to her niece's home nearby. The niece's husband answered the door. The victim was, as you would imagine, in a dishevelled and a distressed state and there were scratches to her face. When she was alone with her niece, she said she had been raped and she was taken to Wimbledon and the suite at that time in use for the victims of sexual assault. There she was examined and various swabs and samples were taken.

'A high vaginal swab appeared to be blood-stained and there was semen present from which a DNA profile – many years later and as a result of the refinements in forensic techniques – was obtained. It matched the reference profile obtained from the defendant following his arrest. The match probability, the statistical probability of obtaining the same result from someone not related to the defendant, is of the order of one in a billion.

'As I have told you, there is no dispute that the semen is the defendant's. He accepts – as of course he really was bound to – that it is his semen. The issue is how it got on a high vaginal swab. Was it, as the prosecution suggest, because it was he who raped Miss A all those years ago or is it possible, as he will say, that he has been the victim of an attempt to frame him instigated by his ex-wife – the woman who left him some 13 years before the attack on Miss A?

'The victim's home was searched by the police and examined by a scene-of-crime examiner. The victim's nightwear was recovered and submitted for examination by forensic scientists. On Miss A's pyjama bottoms, there was a large area of semen staining. Again many years later, a DNA profile was obtained and again that matched the defendant's DNA profile. The match probability figure is in the order of one in a billion.

'Miss A was never to return to the bungalow. She was just too anxious and too insecure to have the confidence to be able to face up to that. She stayed with her niece for the next couple of months before moving to a first-floor flat nearby. In 2005, as I have said, Miss A died.

'Counts 3, 4 and 5: the burglary at Warlingham, and the indecent assault and attempted rape of Mrs B during the night of 4/5 September 1998.

'We move on almost six years to 1998 and to the next of the charged offences committed, suggest the prosecution, by the defendant. Back in 1998, Mrs B was 81 years old. She was not then in good health: she had had both hips replaced, she suffered from chronic arthritis, which made movement very difficult and Mrs B walked with a stick, and was almost housebound. Mrs B died the following June, in 1999.

'Mrs B lived alone in a bungalow in Warlingham, Surrey. She had moved into that address in 1987 with her husband but he had died shortly afterwards and she had lived there alone ever since. Mrs B had a home help and she was also visited by a friend who would shop for her. Because of her mobility problems and in order to give these people easier access to the house, there was a key to the back door kept outside, concealed from view, on a hook on the fence in the alleyway. The defendant, presumably during his reconnaissance, had either discovered this or seen it used and that was the way entry was gained for this particular attack.

'On the Friday night, 4 September 1998, Mrs B went to bed at about 23.30. She was dressed in a nightie and pants. She awoke in the early hours of the morning to find her assailant, the man who was to attempt to rape her, standing over her bed. He was holding her shoulders and Mrs B saw he was wearing a black mask, which covered his face. The defendant asked, "Where's your money? I want your money." He was not aggressive in his tone. Instead, he was calm and in her witness statement the victim described him as speaking nicely. Mrs B said she did not have any money and she began to cry. The defendant put his hand over her mouth and he told her, "Shut up, don't make a noise. Don't tell anybody." He was still speaking in a calm voice. The victim tried again to persuade her attacker to leave her alone. She said, "I think you're thoroughly mean. I am 81, you know, and the shock could do anything." He did not reply but held her face even more tightly.

'The victim then watched as the defendant began a search of the room by torchlight. This took some time and the victim thought it might have been as long as ten minutes before the defendant turned his attention to her. He then pulled the clothing off the bed, took off Mrs B's pants and pulled up her nightie. He got on to the bed and undid his trousers. The defendant then put his fingers into the victim's vagina – that is the charge of indecent assault, count 4 – before then forcing her legs apart, climbing upon her and he tried to penetrate her with his penis. It was not simply a frightening and a degrading experience to which the defendant subjected Mrs B but it was also an incredibly painful one. Because of her chronic arthritis it was extremely difficult for her to open her legs. The defendant was unable to enter Mrs B – which is why the charge, count 5, is one of attempted rape – and, although the victim was to think that he had introduced a cream or some sort of lubricant, in fact as the forensic evidence was to show, he ejaculated between her legs.

'Through the rape, the victim continued in her attempts to dissuade her assailant from continuing with his attack. Although she had stopped her crying out, she feigned chest pains and she began to groan. The defendant shone his torch into her face but continued in his attempts to penetrate her. Only when he had finished did he check her pulse before leaving the address. Although he had carried out a search of the address, he left empty-handed.

'Mrs B then fell asleep. When she awoke she did not, as you might expect, ring for help or for the police immediately. As I am sure you know, victims of violent sexual attacks do not – in a state of shock and in the immediate aftermath of the trauma – always behave as you might expect. It was not until the next evening, when she became frightened she might be attacked again, that she telephoned her son and it was in that way that the police were alerted to what had happened.

'Her description of her assailant again shows how difficult it was for victims of her age, and attacked in this way, to provide reliable or consistent information to the police about the individual they were seeking to identify. Mrs B thought her attacker was 5 feet 5 inches tall, of slender build, in his mid-twenties and thirties. She could not see his face because of the mask he was wearing and she could not say what colour skin he had.

'When Mrs B was examined there was bruising to her neck and right forearm and slight reddening of the vestibule and introitus. Swabs were taken. ... A DNA profile was obtained from the semen, which matched the defendant's DNA profile. The match probability statistic was in the order of one in a billion.

'The examination of the address revealed that the key that had been kept outside was missing. A scene-of-crime officer found that a small window to the victim's bedroom was slightly ajar and there was an indentation to the frame on the outside. Inside, again on the same window frame, there were woollen glove-type marks. Within the address the police recovered a swab from a stain on the bedroom carpet. There was semen present on the swab from which a DNA profile was obtained. The profile was to match the reference profile obtained from the defendant after his arrest and the match probability in this instance was approximately 1 in 23 million.

'Mrs B's nightdress and dressing gown were examined as well. There was a stain on the lower inside back of the nightdress which contained semen. The DNA result was the same as the stain on the floor in the bedroom. So a DNA profile was obtained – it matched the defendant's DNA profile and the match probability was that figure of 1 in 23 million.

'Count 6 and the burglary in Beckenham on the night of 19/20 June 1999; the home of Mrs C.

'Now to the summer of 1999 and the first of a series of seven burglaries committed within the space of a couple of months. Mrs C was, at the time of this burglary, back in June 1999, 71 years old. She lived at a terraced house in Beckenham, a house she had then occupied for the previous 43 years. She lived alone.

'The 19 June was a Saturday and she had gone to bed at about midnight. Sometime later, she was woken by the weight of a man leaning across her body. He had his hand across Mrs C's mouth and nose. The defendant, as the subsequent examination of the address would demonstrate, had entered the house by removing the entire panel of glass from the kitchen window to the rear of the premises. The victim saw that the intruder was dressed in black and his face was covered. Save for the fact that he was a large black male, Mrs C could provide no further description of the defendant.

'With her mouth and nose covered, Mrs C began to struggle but she was no match for the intruder. He then put first one pillow and then another over her face until she stopped her struggling. The defendant said, "Diamonds and money," and the victim said she would get her purse. In fact, the defendant had by that point already found her purse and some jewellery. He then started to search the chest of drawers in the bedroom using a small torch. As he did so, he asked where her husband was. The victim told him that her husband was working in London. That was not true: her husband had died some years earlier.

'At that point, the defendant said, "I want oral sex with you." In an effort to distract the defendant and in the hope she would be able to lock herself in the room, Mrs

C asked to get some water from the bathroom. The defendant followed her along the corridor and then gripped her arm. The victim struck out, attempting to hit the defendant in the genitals. She missed but she did dislodge the torch from his hand. The defendant began searching for the thing: he was obviously anxious to recover it. Mrs C began to plead with the defendant to leave her and he did just that, leaving the house by the kitchen door.

'It was then the victim noticed that the electricity supply to the house had been turned off and the telephone line had been pulled from the receiver in the bedroom. You can see the pattern as to how the defendant committed his offences was beginning to emerge. Without the means of making a call to the police, the victim ran across the road to her neighbours to alert them to the break in.

'A subsequent examination of the house revealed that, during the search the defendant had carried out whilst the victim slept, he had found and stolen valuable diamond rings, a bracelet and approximately £100 in cash. As I have said, entry to the house was gained by removing both the glass and sealant from a window in the kitchen.

'She [Mrs B] was badly bruised on her right arm and had swelling to her nose and cuts to the inside of her mouth.

'During their examination of the scene of this, the third of the offences in this sequence, the police recovered a scarf on a table in the lounge. Scientists examined the item for the presence of body fluids and what was probably saliva was found. This was tested for DNA and a partial profile was obtained which matched the corresponding parts of the defendant's profile. The match probability of a match in an unrelated member of the public would be of the order of one in a billion.

'Count 7: the attempted burglary in Orpington, during July 1999; the home of Mrs D.

'The next of the offences in this series occurred at some point in July. It was not an offence that gave rise to any form of sexual attack or indeed a successful burglary. The defendant was unable on this occasion to break in or, alternatively, perhaps, he was disturbed. Instead, this is an offence linked to the defendant by his use of a particular tool in his attempt to break into the premises. As you will learn, casts or impressions can be taken from marks left by tools such as screwdrivers at the scenes of burglary and, given sufficient detail, tool marks can be compared. Because every tool once used will become marked in an individual way and begin to bear evidence of damage, it is possible, using a microscope, to compare markings.

'This same tool was used on at least three other occasions during that same period: during a burglary and indecent assault in early July (counts 8 to 9), at an address where the defendant committed a burglary and the rape of the occupant in late July (counts 12 to 13) and at an address where, in early August of the same year, the defendant broke into the address and raped and indecently assaulted the occupant (counts 16 to 18).

'Mrs D was then, back in the summer of 1999, 77 years old. She had lived at that address in Orpington since 1988, having moved there with her husband. He died in 1991 and she had lived there ever since on her own.

'On 5 August 1999, police officers investigating the offences which had occurred more recently nearby visited Mrs D at her home and she was able to show them tool marks to the metal frame of the patio doors at the rear of her home. They had the appearance of small gouges, as if someone had tried to force open the door with a screwdriver. Mrs D was able to say that she had first noticed the damage some two to three weeks earlier.

'An identification officer examined the scene on 6 August 1999, and he found marks also to the ground-floor windows at the address. There were scratches on the outside surfaces of one rear and one side window. He also saw the damage to the opening edge and adjacent frame of the rear patio door and made cast impressions.

'Mr John Birkett, a forensic scientist who specialises in the examination of tool marks and from whom you will hear, examined two of the casts and there are "conclusive links" with the tool used at [two addresses] together with a potential – but not conclusive – link to [a third address].

'Counts 8–9: burglary and the indecent assault of Mr E on 3 /4 July 1999.

'That brings us to a bungalow in Coulsdon, the third in this cluster of seven sets of offences committed in the summer of 1999. Mr E is now dead. He died in September

2000, but in July 1999 he was 83 years old. He was in poor health. He was then registered blind, although he had some vision, suffered from Parkinson's Disease and he had some difficulty hearing. The victim did not wish to make a statement, although an account was obtained from him. So this is what he told the police.

'On Saturday, 3 July 1999, Mr E went to bed at about 22.00 and he fell asleep. In the early hours of the morning, now Sunday, 4 July, he was woken by a figure sitting at the foot of his bed, asking him for money. The intruder, this defendant, had a small torch with him. The victim said that he only had £5 and he was then dragged from his bed and frog-marched to the hall where he showed the intruder the money which he kept in a small wooden box. There was £17.

'The defendant took Mr E back to the bedroom where he was struck. The elderly victim fought back and started screaming and then the defendant covered his face with a pillow and inserted his fingers in Mr E's anus. Mr E was able to free himself and his assailant left the room.

'Mr E heard the noise of the defendant searching the house and he lay on the bed pretending to be asleep. He fell asleep and woke again at 04.30, when he tried to use the telephone to call the police but the line was dead. He also discovered that the lights did not work; again the defendant had cut off the electricity supply. The victim called a neighbour who alerted the police to his ordeal.

'Police officers arrived to find the premises in darkness: light bulbs had been removed. Mr E was in a confused and distressed state, and he was tearful and complaining of chest pains.

'Entry had been gained by the removal of a window at the rear of the premises and it was on the beading that the tool marks were found. Mr Birkett has found links between these tool marks and the tools used not just during the previous offence ... but also with the offences of burglary and indecent assault which were committed over three years later in October 2002.

'Following the offences Mr E was examined by a doctor, who found bruising to the right side of the victim's chest and ribs. The upper part of both arms was bruised where he had been held.'

'Counts 10 and 11: the burglary in Addiscombe during the night of 11 July 1999 and the indecent assault of Mrs F.

'At about midnight on Sunday, 11 July 1999, Mrs F, who was then 82 years old – she died in 2004 – went to bed at her home at in Addiscombe. This is a detached two-storey property. She awoke to find an intruder, this defendant, standing over her. He had covered her nose and face with his hand and he was wearing a full-face balaclava, dark clothes and gloves. She asked what he wanted and the defendant said "Money". Mrs F said she would not scream and that the money was in her handbag in the wardrobe. The defendant took his hand from the victim's mouth, found the handbag and took the notes from the victim's purse.

'The defendant then returned to the bed where the victim was now sitting. He sat down next to her and rested his head against hers before asking, "Do you want to have sex?" The victim was so shocked that she asked him to repeat what he had said and she then told him she was an old woman and it wouldn't do anything for either him or her. Nonetheless, the defendant pushed the victim's legs apart, moved her nightdress up and then put his hands between her legs, although he did not actually touch the vaginal area. Mrs F asked him not to hurt her and she describes the intruder's manner as "almost respectful – he was not violent or aggressive". He placed his hands between her legs "and tried to fumble around". She asked him not to hurt her.

'The victim then said she wanted to use the toilet and she was allowed to do so. Having looked into the other rooms, with the use of a torch, the defendant then went downstairs with the victim following him. On the ground floor, the defendant took a can of beer from his pocket, which he drank from. Before leaving the address, he put the can – a can of John Smith's bitter – down. Later, the police would recover it and it is another of the important exhibits, which would reveal trace evidence identifying the defendant as the perpetrator of this particular set of offences.

'Mrs F asked the defendant when he was going to go and she opened the front door. She said, "Thank you for not hurting me," and with that the defendant shook her by the hand, pushed her back from the door and then left, having closed the front door behind him. The victim tried to turn the lights on but discovered that the defendant had previously removed the fuses from the fuse box in the cellar.

'The victim's description of the intruder was that he was 5 feet 7 inches to 5 feet 9 inches tall and athletic to well built. He was so well concealed she could not even see the colour of his skin.

'The examination of the address revealed that the lower panel at the back door had been removed. There were tool marks on the beading, at least one of which had been made by a screwdriver, and matching detail from the same screwdriver was found at the next set of offences, counts 12 and 13.

'The beer can was found on the ground-floor hall table and the area around the opening was swabbed for DNA: various components but not the defendant's entire DNA was recovered. It is not possible to ascribe a statistical match probability to a result of this sort.

'Counts 12–13: the burglary in Addiscombe on 29 July 1999 and the rape of Mrs G.

'Mrs G was 82 years old in 1999. She died in December 2007. Mrs G had moved into her home in Addiscombe shortly after her marriage in 1944 and she had lived there with her husband and their children ever since. Her husband died in 1978 and the last of the children left home in 1982, so since that date she had been living alone at that address. The house was a semi-detached property with two floors.

'At about 22.15 on Wednesday, 28 July 1999, Mrs G got herself ready for bed. At about 02.00 she woke to use the toilet and then she went back to sleep. A little later she woke, having heard the noise of the living-room door being opened. Mrs G got up to investigate and as she went into the living room she was grabbed and a hand was put over her mouth, presumably to stop her screaming out. The hand was a gloved one. The victim describes herself in the witness statement made to the police as too frightened to think but she said, "I'm 82, what do you want with me?" The defendant said, "Money," and moved her back towards the bedroom where she had been sleeping. There, Mrs G found her handbag and gave it to the defendant. He took the notes from it.

'The defendant then turned his attention to his elderly victim. He pushed her back on to the bed and then tried to undo the buttons on her nightie before pulling it apart. He then put his hands inside and rubbed the victim's breasts. It was, as the victim described it, "horrible". The defendant then removed Mrs G's pants and he began to try to kiss her. He told the victim to kiss him and then asked her to remove her dentures. Then he put his fingers into her vagina in an attempt to moisten her before raping her.

'Following the attack the defendant, who by now was obviously becoming aware of the developments in forensic science and the use to which DNA profiling evidence was beginning to be put in the criminal courts, told Mrs G to take her nightdress off. She asked why and he explained, "There's semen on it." Then, having searched the house, the defendant left. Before he left, the victim asked him why he had done it and he replied that he would never do it again. With him gone, the victim discovered that the defendant had soaked her nightdress in a bowl in the sink.

'Again, the defendant's practice of carrying out attacks at night and whilst masked was almost to remove the possibility of any of his victims identifying him. Mrs G's description of him is of a man taller than her (she was 5 feet 1 inch), black but not very dark-skinned. He had a balaclava, gloves and also a torch.

'The scene-examiners were to find that entry had been gained through a kitchen window. The lower part of the window had been removed from the frame and was found in the garden. The window beading was examined and there were a series of tool marks including some which had been made by a screwdriver or some similar implement which had also been used at the earlier offences.

'The victim was examined by a doctor who found a bruise on her left elbow and a red mark on her right arm. Petechiae [small spots caused by bleeding into the skin] on her inner lower lip was consistent with injury from a hand over her mouth, and her vaginal injuries are suggestive of attempted penile penetration of the vagina.

'The water in the bowl in which the defendant had soaked the dress was sampled and semen was recovered. The DNA profile obtained matched the defendant's and the match probability was of the order of one in a billion.

'High and low vaginal swabs recovered from the victim also revealed semen. This for testing purposes was combined with the low vaginal swab and submitted for DNA testing. A partial profile from the semen matched the defendant's and the match probability was in the region of one in 77 million.

'Counts 14–15: the burglary on 4 August 1999, and the indecent assault on Mrs H.

'The address is a detached bungalow situated in a cul-de-sac. Mrs H, who died in October 2007, was living there alone. She had moved to the address with her husband some 40 years earlier and had continued to live there after her husband's death 16 years later. She was 88 years old at the time of these offences.

'She went to bed at about 23.45 on Tuesday, 3 August 1999. She was wearing a vest and a cotton nightdress. At about 03.00 the following morning, she was woken by being shaken by the shoulder. There was a black man standing over her. Her description of him, for what it is worth, is black, clean-shaven, oblong puffy face with a forceful look. He was about 40 years old, thick-set and strong looking. Her intruder was holding a torch and shining it in her face. The intruder, the defendant, then removed the bulb from the bedside lamp.

'The victim looked at the defendant and asked him, "What do you want? How did you get in?" The defendant then pulled the sheet off Mrs H, grabbed her arm and put her hand on to his penis, which by that stage was out of his trousers. The victim pulled her hand away. Whether she said anything at this point is unclear; she may have said something to the effect of "It is a good job your mother can't see you now." In any event he took his attempts to get her to masturbate him no further and instead turned his attention to searching the bedroom. Having done that, he left.

'After the victim had reported the incident to the police, the search of the address was to reveal that the defendant had gained entry to the bungalow by removing one of the lounge windows to the rear of the premises. He had also cut the telephone line. Inside the address, the defendant had plainly made a search of the other rooms before he had woken Mrs H. Amongst the exhibits recovered from the address was a miniature Campari bottle from which it appeared the intruder had drunk.

'The window unit and the pieces of beading were examined and casts of the tool marks were taken. The marks had been made by at least one screwdriver and the microscopic examination showed clear links with the offences committed the previous month, with the offence we come to next and also an offence the defendant would commit three years later.

'A DNA profile was obtained from the rim of the Campari bottle. It matched the reference profile obtained from the defendant and the match probability is in the order of one in one billion.

'Counts 16–18: the burglary on 5 August 1999 and the indecent assault and rape of Mrs I.

'The last of the series of seven sets of offences committed during the summer of 1999 was carried out by the defendant at the Orpington home of Mrs I. She is now dead – she died in September 2006 – but back in August 1999 she was 88 years old. She had been living in Orpington, in a bungalow, since 1974. She lived alone; her second husband had died in 1967. Although she suffered from arthritis and she was not as mobile as she had been, up until this attack upon her, Mrs I had been able to lead a largely independent and fulfilling life.

'Late on Wednesday, 4 August 1999, she went to bed in the bedroom in the front of the premises. At about 03.00, now on 5 August, she was woken by a noise and she saw a figure standing at the foot of her bed. The intruder, the defendant, is described as being completely covered from head to foot in what she describes as a cat-type suit. He was wearing a balaclava, gloves and he had a torch which he shone into her eyes. He then covered the victim's face and mouth with his hand and whispered, "Don't scream, I won't hurt you." She asked what he wanted and he whispered, "Money."

'She told the intruder there was no money in the bedroom and that her purse was in the living room. The defendant pulled the elderly lady to her feet. She managed to grab hold of her walking stick and he pushed her into the living room, where he sat her down in an armchair. There she took up her handbag and gave the defendant her purse.

'The defendant, having taken cash from the purse, turned his attention to the victim. He first took her out of the armchair, dragged her across to the settee and then positioned the victim so she was sitting on the edge of this piece of furniture. The defendant proceeded next to pull up her nightdress and he attempted to rape her. [Mr Laidlaw then described in detail the attack and the Stalker's acts towards the elderly lady up until the point that the assailant went into the bathroom having 'satisfied him'.]

'The defendant returned into the lounge,' Mr Laidlaw continued. 'He threw the victim a towel and then began frantically searching for something. Mrs I asked what he was looking for and he said it was his glove. The victim was to find that for him and with that he then left the premises. At 03.37, Mrs I managed to alert Carelink via an intercom system installed at the address.

'Both the police and paramedics from the ambulance service went to the scene. Mrs I had been seriously injured and she was taken to hospital, where she was to undergo surgery for tears to her vagina and damage to her abdominal cavity. There was also damage to the surface of the rectum. It was not just serious physical injury that the victim suffered. She was never to return to her home but instead she moved into sheltered accommodation, where she was to stay until she died in 2006. She was to continue to suffer the psychological impact of the defendant's attack.

'The police discovered in their examination and

search of the address that the defendant had once again gained entry to the home of one of his victims by the removal of a window. ... It was the entire window from the kitchen at the rear of the address which had been taken out. Beading from that window was to reveal the same markings as were discovered at four of the other of the summer 1999 offences and the October 2002 offence committed.

'The nightdress worn by Mrs I was examined and semen was detected on the lower front near the hem. A DNA profile was obtained from the semen, which matched the defendant's profile, and the match probability was in the order of one in a billion. There was also a trace of semen found on one of the brown cushions.

'That therefore is the last of the summer 1999 offences and we move next, in the series of offences with which the defendant is charged, to October 2002.

'Counts 19–20: in Shirley on 13 October 2002 and the indecent assault upon Miss J.

'The house in Shirley, in Kent, is a detached, two-storey property. It was the home of Miss J, who was then 77 years old. The house had been her parents' and she had lived there alone, as a spinster, since their deaths. Miss J went to bed at about 22.45 on Saturday, 12 October 2002 before sometime later, in the early hours of the Sunday morning, she was woken. Miss J took out a torch she kept under her pillow and she saw there was an intruder in her room. Her description of the defendant was about 5 feet

9 inches tall, burly build, with a light black skin. He had a south London accent.

'The defendant approached Miss J and he said something like, "I want to tie you up." He then got on top of her and placed his hand over her mouth. Miss J bit him and felt that he was wearing gloves. The defendant also had a torch, which he shone into her face. He was very aggressive and he was pushing down upon the victim with all his body weight. The defendant tried next to kiss the victim and he forced his tongue into her mouth. He was also trying to prise her legs apart and Miss J feared she was about to be raped. It was as the victim described it, "an awful dream".

'Miss J is a brave and spirited woman because, despite the ordeal, she kept her legs closed and she began her attempts to push him away. She also began speaking to him, a dialogue she was to keep up until the defendant left the address. She told him to get off and, although the defendant said words such as "fuck" and also, at one point, he seemed to be saying that she should go and wash herself, the victim pretended not to be able to hear and eventually the defendant gave up. Whilst scared, as I have told you, that she was about to be raped, her spirited resistance was successful.

'The victim did, however, say that the defendant could have money and she produced her purse which she also kept under her pillow whilst she slept. At this, the defendant appeared to become less aggressive and he allowed Miss J to get up. She then accompanied him around the house as he looked for money and other valuables to steal. Her dialogue continued and eventually she was also successful in persuading the defendant to leave the address. Before he left, he kissed the victim on her cheek and she promised not to call the police for ten minutes.

'The police arrived at the address at shortly after 04.00. They found that the electricity supply to the address had been shut off by the intruder at the master switch. Entry had been gained by the removal of a window at the rear of the premises and the beading was recovered for further scientific examination. Within the house, the police discovered that light bulbs had been removed and the telephone wire in the hallway had been cut. It was an offence bearing all the hallmarks of this defendant's particular method of offending and carrying out his attacks.

'Several pieces of the beading were examined and the tool marks found provide clear links with four of the summer 1999 offences. ... Apart from the links provided by the tools being used by the defendant, there is also DNA evidence which shows it was he and nobody else who was responsible for the attack upon Miss J. When the police learned that the perpetrator had kissed the victim, they swabbed Miss J's cheeks for body fluid. It would have to be saliva and from the swabs DNA was recovered.

'The result was what is referred to by that expert as a mixed result, but all the components of the defendant's

DNA can be seen in the result and of the following two propositions, first, that this was a mixture of DNA from the defendant and the victim or, secondly, that the mixture of DNA comes from someone unrelated to the defendant and Miss J, the DNA profiling results are approximately 64 million times more likely if the first proposition was true rather than the second.

'Count 21: the burglary in West Dulwich on 8 March 2003.

'We move on almost six months in time to March 2003 and to the next of the offences with which the defendant is charged, the burglary at the home of Mrs K.

'Mrs K was then aged 78 and the house in West Dulwich, an end-of-terrace property, had been the home of she and her husband since 1964 when it was built by the council. Mrs K's husband died in August 1995 and from that date she had lived at the address alone. The victim suffered from sciatica and she had some support from a home help. Otherwise, although she walked with the help of a stick, she was able to lead an independent life.

'On the night of Friday, 7 March 2003, she went to bed at about 23.00. She woke at about 02.00 and then noticed the light on the landing go out. As she took up her stick and began to make her way slowly downstairs to investigate, Mrs K also saw that the lights on the telephone receiver were no longer illuminated. The electricity supply had been turned off. In the hallway, as she searched for her torch, she suddenly became aware of the intruder: as she put it, a "huge black figure" looming over her.

'The defendant then pushed the old lady to the ground and he was over her, with his hand covering her mouth. Mrs K thought he was 5 feet 10 inches tall, of quite broad build. He was wearing dark clothing, wearing a balaclava and he was gloved. At first, Mrs K tried to fight her way free but she was simply no match for the defendant and her stick was trapped beneath her. She decided it was better not to struggle and she asked what he wanted. The defendant replied, "Money," and she pointed out where her handbag was on a table in the hallway. He took the notes from her purse and as he searched the bag the victim asked him to help her get up. This the defendant did and, when Mrs K asked if she could sit in the lounge, the defendant helped her into that room. He was, as the victim describes him, considerate. There she waited while the defendant went upstairs to search the rooms there.

'The defendant then returned and with a cloth he began carefully to wipe Mrs K's hands. It is another example, as the years passed, both of the defendant obviously having become conscious of the developments in forensic science and of the care he displayed in order to avoid detection. Having wiped both the hands and the fingernails, the defendant allowed Mrs K to go upstairs before he left the address. When she tried to call the police, she found the telephone had been disconnected. The power had been switched off at the fuse box.

'Police discovered that entry had been gained by the

dining-room window to the rear of the premises, the window having been removed. It was found placed against the wall of the house.

'Fingernail scrapings were taken from Mrs K and, despite the defendant's best efforts, it was these which provide another forensic link to him. Again, a mixed DNA profile was obtained, the major part of which matched the reference profile from the victim. The minor was consistent with the defendant's profile. Of the two propositions, that is that the mixture came from Mrs K and Delroy Grant, or alternatively, it was a mixture of DNA from Mrs K and an unknown male unrelated to the defendant, the scientist has concluded the DNA profiling result is approximately 16 million times more likely if the first proposition was true rather than the second.

'Count 22: the burglary in Bromley on 8 September 2004, the home of Mrs L.

'Now, 18 months on, and to September 2004, and the burglary in a semi-detached, three-bedroom house, the home of Mrs L. She was then 84 years old and she lived alone, having been widowed some years earlier.

'Mrs L went to bed at about midnight on 6 September before she was woken by sounds at about 01.00, now 7 September 2004. She dozed for the next hour or so until she woke at about 02.00 when a gloved hand was placed over her face. There was a figure standing over her. He was wearing gloves and carrying a torch.

'The defendant told her not to scream and he asked,

"Where's the money?" He was quietly spoken. Mrs L asked to be allowed to get up and she said, "Don't hurt me, please don't hurt me." The defendant then searched the bedroom until the victim asked to use the toilet. The defendant followed her, instructing her not to put the lights on. As she emerged from the toilet, the defendant pushed the victim and she grazed her arm, which started to bleed. Mrs L said she would have to put a plaster on it and this, too, he allowed her to do.

'Downstairs at the house, the defendant again asked for money and Mrs L showed him her savings, about £1,000 in cash, concealed in a drawer in the kitchen. It was money saved from her pension and intended to be used to pay for new windows. The defendant then left the address, telling his victim not to call the police. In fact, it was her neighbours who Mrs L was to go to for help.

'The police arrived at 03.36. They found, consistent with the clear pattern of this defendant's method of operation, that he had gained entry by removing a window at the rear of the property. He had also cut the telephone line to the address. Inside a bulb from the bedside lamp had been removed.

'The surrounding area was searched and an important exhibit again providing, so the prosecution suggest, cogent evidence was recovered. This was a black woollen glove which, when examined in conjunction with other of the exhibits recovered and associated with the burglary, provided a number of links between the defendant and this offending.

'First, from inside the glove at the base of the first finger, the scientists recovered DNA. It was a mixture of DNA within which there were all the components of the defendant's DNA and all those of a woman called Barbara Stocks, with whom the defendant at the time of his arrest was involved in a relationship. The match probability of that mixture being another male's DNA who was unrelated to the defendant and another girl unrelated to his girlfriend is in the region of one in one billion. So this is consistent with the glove having been an article used by one or both the defendant and Miss Stocks or at the address they shared. So the glove found close to the scene of the burglary is plainly linked to the defendant.

'Now to the links with the offence. Inside the bathroom, the police found a pair of green trousers. Fibres from these trousers were found on the gloves. On the beading from the window which had been removed by the burglar there were also fibres both from the gloves and the green trousers. Finally, on Mrs L's nightdress the police found fibres both from the gloves and the trousers. The intruder had obviously been wearing the gloves, which have that very strong DNA link to the defendant and his girlfriend.

'Count 23: the burglary in Bromley on 25 May 2009, the home of Mr M.

'We move now to 2009 and the final seven offences in this long sequence with which the defendant is charged. So these are offences committed in the final six months before his arrest in November 2009.

'The first is the burglary in Bromley, Kent, which is at a three-bedroom, semi-detached house. It was the home of Mr M, who was then 62 years old, and his elderly mother and another suffer of dementia. On the Sunday night, so the night of 24 May 2009, Mr M had gone to bed at about 22.00. He had left a carton of orange juice, unopened, on the side in the kitchen. In the early hours of the Sunday morning, he woke to find that the house had been burgled. The room where he mother slept had been searched, as had the rooms downstairs, and money had been stolen. On this occasion, was it because the defendant must have seen two people in the premises that he had not attempted to wake either occupant and had satisfied himself with just the money?

'Entry had been gained by forcing a kitchen window. Consistent with the defendant's method of operation, the telephone cable had also been cut. The damage to the window was examined and casts of the marks caused by the tool used to force the window were made. In due course, the forensic scientists would establish that it was a screwdriver recovered during a burglary on 6 June 2009 which had been used. There was also DNA on the screwdriver. Again, it was a mixed result but the majority of the defendant's components were found amongst the mixture.

'But that was not the only evidential link between the burglary and this defendant. The carton of orange juice left by Mr M in the kitchen had been opened and the burglar had drunk from it. It was sampled for DNA to see whether there might be any clue to be gained from any saliva left upon it. There was DNA present. It was a partial profile but it matched the defendant and the match probability of obtaining the same result from another not related to him was in the order of one in one billion.

'Count 24: the burglary in South Croydon on 6 June 2009, the home of Mrs N.

'This is the home of Mrs N, who lives alone, and was 82 years old when her semi-detached, three-bedroom home was burgled. Although it is clear the defendant gained entry, he does not appear to have taken anything from the address. Perhaps he was disturbed or unsettled. Mrs N has Alzheimer's and she is frail, and she could only provide a vague account of what happened. She spoke, when talking to the police, of having woken to see a man looking through the cupboard drawers in her bedroom and then of this man being in her bed. The police asked if he had touched her but he said that he had not.

'Later that morning, between 07.00 and 07.30, Mrs N telephoned her daughter to say she had been burgled. The daughter went to the address and found that a pane of glass had been removed from the kitchen window and inside the house the telephone cable had been cut. The screwdriver had been forced into the fence outside and left there.

'On this occasion, shoe marks were recovered at the scene. These were consistent with having been made by a pair of training shoes that were found at the defendant's home following his arrest.

'Counts 25–26: the burglary in Thornton Heath on 13 August 2009 and the indecent assault of Mr O.

'The offence committed in August 2009 is the first of the final series of offences where the evidential links to this defendant arise from the vehicle he was found to be driving when he was arrested – a grey Vauxhall Zafira car – and to property and clothing found within it.

'The house is a three-bedroom, semi-detached house and the home of Mr O. He was 88 years old and he lived alone. He had been the victim of another burglary in 1 June 2009, which you need to have in mind because it will make sense of what happened. At about 02.00 in the morning of Thursday, 13 August 2009, Mr O was disturbed by sounds in the house and he began to investigate. As he came down the stairs from the first floor, he was confronted by the defendant, "a black figure climbing the staircase", as the victim described him. Thinking he must be the June burglar, the victim said, "Oh hello. Well, we meet again."

'The defendant was masked, his clothing was black and he was wearing gloves. He was, according to the victim, about 5 feet 9 inches in height and quite slim. Mr O thought he was an Indian man. The defendant spoke quietly and led Mr O back to his bedroom where he told the victim to undress. The defendant helped the victim to take off his clothes and he removed everything apart from his socks. The victim thought he was about to be killed, that the intruder would produce a knife and he prayed for a quick death.

'But then the defendant started to pull at the old man's nipples, he rubbed at his stomach and handled his penis. When the victim did not become erect, the defendant asked him, "Are you scared?" and "Are you nervous?" Next the defendant led his victim to the bathroom, went himself to the toilet and then he told Mr O to dress.

'The defendant then took the old man downstairs where the victim gave the defendant what money he had, only £15. The defendant became more aggressive at that point and he said he knew the householder had more. Mr O reached out for his purse, which the defendant grabbed. From that he took £45 and a debit card, a Barclaycard Visa card. He asked for the PIN number. Mr O had the presence of mind to give him a four-digit number but not for that card: it was in fact the directory enquiries number for the partially sighted. The defendant then continued his search on the ground floor before leaving the house. On his way out, he touched the victim on the shoulder and said, "We're still good friends."

'The precautions the defendant had taken to prevent any possibility of the householder calling the police were as before and these represent both his hallmark and the care in planning and committing the offences. On this occasion, the cable had been pulled from the telephone receiver. The police were called.

'Now to the defendant's use of the stolen debit card and

the links to the Vauxhall Zafira. Banking records show there was an unsuccessful attempt made to use the card at a Lloyds TSB ATM at 364 Lordship Lane in East Dulwich at 03.13 that morning, but there is no CCTV coverage in that immediate area. Just a few minutes later, at 03.38am, the defendant's Vauxhall Zafira arrived at the Shell garage at 163–165 Stanstead Road, Forest Hill, which is just to the south of the defendant's home. The film from the garage is of sufficient quality to identify the car as a Vauxhall Zafira and the pictures of the driver are certainly of the defendant.

'Then, about 15 minutes later, there was a second attempt to use Mr O's debit card at an ATM at Gogi's off-licence at 60 Honor Oak Park at 03.54.34 and 03.54.56. There are CCTV cameras in that area and you will note how the defendant had dressed to use the ATM. [Mr Laidlaw then referred to one of the photographic documents the jury had.]

'He knew perfectly well, having committed this long catalogue of offences that the police would seek to recover any film from CCTV cameras providing coverage of ATMs where cards stolen during his offences were used. He was plainly doing all he could to frustrate any identification of him. In fact, however, the blue cagoule he had worn with its hood pulled up and over his face would be recovered by the police from the Vauxhall Zafira on his arrest in November. DNA consistent with being the defendant's was recovered upon it.

'Count 27: the burglary in Forest Hill on 18 October 2009, the home of Mrs P.

'The semi-detached in Forest Hill is the home of Mrs P, 87 years old when the defendant burgled her. She is a widow and she had lived alone at the address since the death of her husband.

'On 17 October 2009, a Saturday, the victim went to bed at about 23.00. At sometime after about 02.45, she awoke. She switched her bedside light on to find an intruder in her bedroom: he was wearing dark-coloured clothes and his face was covered and he was wearing gloves. The victim thought the intruder was 5 feet 10 inches to 6 feet tall and well built. He was shining a torch into the victim's eyes.

'The defendant began to search the drawers of a bedside cabinet. Mrs P told him, "I've had a few burglars and I haven't got anything left. The only thing I have got is some jewellery which is in the bottom drawer at the back." The defendant stood up and he had Mrs P's Barclaycard debit card in his hand. She told him to take it.

'The defendant then pulled back the covers on the bed and touched Mrs P's nightie around the top of her thighs but he did not make contact with her body. The victim describes the defendant's touch as "gentle and controlled". The defendant then replaced the bedclothes before leaving the room to continue his search elsewhere.

'When he returned, the defendant helped Mrs P up and led her to another room on the first floor, over the garage.

There he provided her with paper and, although he did not speak, it was clear he wanted the PIN number for the card. Mrs P provided him with the correct number and he walked out of the room and left the address.

'Again, when the house was examined by the police, it was to display the hallmarks of the defendant's particular method of offending. There had been attempts to force windows at the back of the premises and inside the address light bulbs had been removed and the cable from the telephone in the bedroom had been pulled out. The tool marks at the rear of the address had been made by a crowbar which would be found in the boot of the Vauxhall Zafira when the defendant was arrested on 15 November.

'Again, on his way home, the defendant was to make attempts to withdraw money using the card stolen from Mrs P. There were four attempts to use the card between 05.26 and 05.28 at the post office in Honor Oak Park and then, again at 05.44, at Gogi's off-licence, 60 Honor Oak Park. Although he had been provided on this occasion with the correct PIN number, he failed to successfully withdraw any money.

'The cameras in the vicinity of Gogi's off-licence show the figure using the ATM. Identification of the defendant is, of course, impossible but a hat and a fleece of the sort that that figure was wearing were recovered from the Zafira after the defendant's arrest. DNA testing on the two exhibits gave results consistent with the defendant's DNA being on both the hat and the fleece.

'One final link between the offence and the defendant.

In the car, the police recovered a torch. DNA testing produced a complex result showing the presence of DNA from at least four people. But there were two components which are extremely rare – in fact, not previously been seen in any of the DNA frequency databases used by the Forensic Science Service. Both components were found in the profile of the victim, Mrs P.

'On the strap or the lanyard of the torch, the scientists were also to recover DNA. It was a complex mixture but it is consistent with representing DNA from both the defendant and the woman, Barbara Stocks, with whom, in 2009, the defendant was then involved.

'Count 28: the burglary in Shirley on 29 October 2009.

'The house is a two-bedroom chalet bungalow where Mrs Q, then 82 years old, lived. She had lived at the address with her husband since 1953, but he had died just a few months before the burglary so she was alone at the address. Mrs Q went to bed on the night of Wednesday, 28 October at about 22.00 and she fell asleep. At what must have been about 03.45, she was woken by an intruder.

'The defendant had broken into her home by forcing a kitchen window at the rear of the property. He then made his way into her bedroom on the ground floor and Mrs Q was awoken by him asking, "Where's the money?" He kept repeating the question but Mrs Q told him she did not have any. Then suddenly it went quiet and he was gone.

'The defendant had taken her handbag, which contained money and her bankcards. There are CCTV cameras at a school nearby and also at an address nearby, and it is film from these which show, from about 03.36, what is believed to be the defendant's Vauxhall Zafira in the area of Mrs Q's home, then being parked nearby before a figure at 03.42 walked towards it.

'Count 29: the attempted burglary in Shirley on 14 November 2009.

'This is the offence which was to lead to the defendant's arrest. First, a word about the premises he targeted on this occasion before I set out for you how it was that the police caught him.

'Mrs R was 86 years old in November of 2009 and she lived alone in a large detached house. She had been at the address for many years, since 1957. Her husband died in 1990 and she had been on her own since then. Mrs R is confined to a wheelchair and cannot cope without help. She slept in a room on the ground floor at the address. At about 19.30 on Saturday, 14 November carers put her to bed and at about 22.00 a neighbour called round to check she was all right.

'Later that night, at just before midnight, police officers on surveillance duties – as part of the operation designed to catch the perpetrator of this long series of offences – saw the defendant running along and then watched as he got into his Vauxhall Zafira. The vehicle, as you will hear when I turn to the arrest, was then followed away from the area. In Witham Road in Beckenham, it was stopped.

'Quite what it was that caused the defendant to abandon his attempt to break into Mrs R's home is not clear. But after his arrest a police search dog trained to track human scent was dispatched to the area, where it picked up a trail from the point where the defendant's car had been parked. This the dog followed back to Mrs R's and the dog stopped beneath the bay window. She had been entirely unaware of the defendant's plans to break into her house. But when the police examined the address they found that the putty to one of the windows in the front bay window had been removed. As I say, why he had abandoned his attempt to burgle Mrs R's home is not clear.

'The defendant's arrest, the search of the Vauxhall Zafira and the interviews.

'The Vauxhall Zafira driven away was followed north and back towards the defendant's home by unmarked police vehicles. In Witham Road in Beckenham at what must have been about 00.15 it was stopped. By then, it was 15 November 2009.

'The defendant was to give his name first as Kelvin Grant but when told there were bank cards in the car in a different name he then gave the name of Delroy Easton. He was asked why he had been out and he pretended that he had been trying to buy cannabis. The defendant was handcuffed and he was searched. In his pocket the police recovered the torch which had been used in the burglary of Mrs P's home the previous month.

'Elsewhere in the car was the crowbar used in the same burglary, the blue cagoule worn by the defendant when he attempted to withdraw money using Mr O's card following the burglary in August, and the fleece and thick dark woolly hat he had worn when attempting to use the bank card stolen from Mrs P's home in October.

'Following his arrest the defendant was cautioned. He made no reply and he was taken to Lewisham police station for the purposes of interview. At the police station, a sample of DNA was taken and his clothing was seized. He had been wearing two pairs of jeans, two pairs of boxer shorts, three T-shirts, a pair of black shoes but no socks.

'At the police station, the defendant's fingerprints were taken. The officer told him, "I am making sure I get ink all over your hands to get a good print from you," to which the defendant replied, "I don't know why you're bothering – I always wear gloves."

'He was interviewed on and between 15 and 18 November 2009. Let me summarise the position he took then and what little it was that he had to say. There was no mention whatsoever, as I have said, of the defence we understand he is to run before you.

'The defendant gave his address as 19 Brockley Mews – a property he shared with two of his children and his wife, a woman called Jennifer Grant. He told the police that he had been born in Jamaica and came to this country when he was 12. As for the offences, when the police turned to question him about them, the defendant made no comment.

'Later in the interviews, the police asked the defendant about a pawnbrokers' receipt for two rings dated 9 June 2009, which had been found at his home. It related to rings, and you will remember amongst the property stolen was jewellery. The defendant accepted he pawned the rings but said he could not remember how he came by them.

'There was a further interview on 3 February 2010. Again, he made no comment to the questions asked of him on that occasion.

'Just one more thing in respect of his detention at Lewisham police station in November 2009 following his charge. On 19 November, an officer went to the defendant's cell to provide him with deodorant. He seemed agitated: he was pacing his cell and he said, "I do not want to fit anyone up." Asked what he meant, the defendant said, "Have you thought about my son? Delroy Junior." The officer asked why he thought his son might be responsible, the defendant said, "He lives in the right area and he is the same height as me." When told that that information would have to be passed on, he said, "No, don't pass it on. I don't want to fit anyone up."'

It was a bravura performance by Mr Laidlaw spread over two days, and when he sat down the case against Delroy

Grant was in the open for all the world to read about and hear. But there were many more surprises in store before the case came to its end.

CHAPTER TWELVE

Delroy Grant and his defence team did not dispute that the appalling crimes on the charge sheet had taken place. They simply said that Grant had not committed them. There was therefore no need to call any surviving victims to cross-examine them to establish the actual events of the night they were raided: it was now purely a matter of proving that Grant had been involved in them.

First, the statements of the nine victims involved in the years up to 1999 – Miss A to Mrs I – were read to the jury by the prosecuting counsel, Mr Laidlaw. Most of these unfortunate elderly people had since died, but their statements about the night their homes were broken into – and the effects that the Night Stalker had had on their lives – remained. The effect of this, however, was that so far the victims of the Night Stalker had had their stories delivered 'from beyond the grave'. It's a ghastly, ghostly phrase that, no matter how well intentioned, somehow ill befits the passing of those victims whose lives had been so cruelly disrupted and ravaged.

But not all the Stalker's victims fell into that category. One of them was Miss J, the woman who, in October 2002, had been the victim of the burglary and indecent assault at her home in Shirley – counts 19 and 20 of the charges the jury were trying. Shortly after the attack, she had been filmed as she was questioned by police about her ordeal. That footage was now shown to the court as the prosecution case continued. Her account was not simply recounted from sheets of paper: the jury could see and hear her living, moving narrative of a night of terror and humiliation on screens in the courtroom.

The white-haired woman, 77 at the time of the raid, had been filmed in a room at Mayday Hospital where she was receiving treatment after the attack. She told officers how she put her light out at about 10.45pm. There was street lighting outside her bedroom so the room was never terribly dark, she said, but 'something must have distracted me because I reached for the little torch I keep under my pillow'.

There was a man in her room. 'I was flabbergasted. I just could not understand how he had got in and I kept asking that. He told me that he had got in with a key.'

Miss J gave the intruder a £10 and £5 note and some loose change. Then things got physical. 'He was wrestling me and I kept pushing him. You begin to think this is an awful dream.' He kept leaning against her and she kept pushing him away. 'I am sure he did not put his whole heart in it as he did not overpower me. He could have brought a knife out.'

She added, 'When I saw him I wondered if this was real. He kept telling me to lie back while pushing me back and I kept telling him, "Get away!" ... I wanted to get up off the bed because I thought he was going to rape me.'

As they grappled, he tried to force her legs apart. 'You get a rush of blood. I did not stop talking and I think he got fed up with me.

'I was semi-prone and he was around the side. I could see his face on a level with mine. His hands were trying to keep me down and I was pushing him away.'

Under gentle questioning from the police, she continued, saying that he had tried to put his tongue in her mouth. 'It was not ferocious. ... I was so angry really, I pushed him away. He said he was going to tie me up, but he never did. I certainly heard tie me up.' She said she also heard him say the word 'fuck' in one context, but she couldn't say exactly what.

Eventually, she said to him, '"If I give you the money, will you go away?" and I got the impression he sort of agreed with that.

'He was fairly calm about it all. He looked at the wardrobe and I thought, "If you look up there, you'll be covered in dust." He was a little bit random but he was not in a hurry.'

They went downstairs and at that time his victim did not have her spectacles on. 'That's like losing my right hand to me,' she said. He had a torch with him 'not much thicker than a fountain pen'. She told her attacker, 'I can give you what I have got here. It isn't very much but then you must go.' She gave him about £60 and then he started to look in her drawers. 'There was a load of tat in there,' she said to the police. She told the intruder, 'You are not keeping your part of the bargain.'

He examined a little transistor radio that had seen better days and had a broken handle. 'I said, "You don't want that, do you?"' Then he looked at her music cabinet, but he didn't seem to know what a record player was, even though she said to him, 'If you want any vinyl records, they are there.' She told the Stalker there was no television in the house as 'I don't have any modern gadgets.'

At one stage, she was afraid he would shut her in the small cupboard where she kept her ironing board but eventually he left, giving her a kiss in the kitchen before he did so and telling her not to phone the police for ten minutes. 'By the time he had left, we had established some sort of rapport. The kiss on the cheek was the nearest he got to being affectionate.'

A year after the attack, Miss J made a statement describing in detail how it had left an indelible mark on her. 'This incident has affected me in various ways that I shall try to describe in this statement. It is something that I shall never forget completely. It still feels so recent. I feel a huge amount of resentment and wonder how the suspect chose me. I often think to myself: "Why me?" or "Why any of the other victims?" I also feel a sense of indignation and anger, as I feel that I had done everything reasonable to avoid this sort of thing happening.

'I am aware that the police have sought advice from academics about the behaviour of the suspect and I really don't agree he does not know he harms. I also don't believe he loves his victims as has been suggested. I believe he knows what he does is wrong because he makes a point of doing it at night. I wouldn't mind talking to these academics and telling them what I think about it.

'I have found that time is not a great healer. I don't think that it has got any easier over the last year. I certainly haven't got back my peace of mind. Nobody can guarantee that it won't happen again. The only reassurance that I can be given is knowing that the suspect is no longer at large.

'Since the incident, in about December 2002, I have found myself increasingly covered in a sort of rash and been seeing a dermatologist from Guy's Hospital about this complaint, which has been diagnosed as endogenous eczema. I had previously seen him for other skin complaints. I did not have eczema before this incident happened. It has got worse over the last year and has crept upwards from my ankles to all over my body. I have to put creams on it and one is so strong that it has to be supervised by the doctor. I originally thought that it was due to the heat at my sister's house, but I have been told that this probably wasn't the cause. I believe that it may have been caused by the anxiety in my life over the last year.

'After the incident, I moved out of the house because the

police needed to do some forensic work there. I moved into my sister's house nearby. I stayed there until the police left my house. Whilst I was there I found myself very security-conscious and locked and bolted everything. I didn't want to go back to my house until it was secure. This didn't happen for about ten days because one of the windows needed boarding up. I wasn't too bothered about going back into the house at that time.

'Once everything was secured and the police had all left, I moved back into my home. I found myself gradually feeling depressed. I felt really low and didn't really want to spend Christmas on my own in the house. I moved back into my sister's house for a while, but they were going away for New Year and I didn't want to stay there alone so I went back home again.

'Another reason I went back home was that the police had installed an alarm there shortly after the incident and this gave me a great sense of security. I arranged for security companies to come round and talk to me about alarm security systems, but in the end I decided that these were not the answer. I have always been quite security conscious anyway but think that I am not pretty neurotic about it. I think my family are foolhardy about it, but they have only ever had property stolen from their house. I have had more than that. I don't care what happens while I am out. It's what happens while I am there that matters.

'After the alarm salesman, I realised that nobody could provide me with the security that I needed and decided to move house. I remember seeing a new block of flats being built and thought that this was the answer, so I put my house on the market and it sold fairly quickly. I had to dispose of a lot of my furniture that belonged to my parents and I also threw away a lot of stuff too. Most of it went to charity. In a way, I resent having to do all this over the last year. I had had years of acquiring things in that house and didn't want to get rid of it all. The purchase of the new flat hasn't gone smoothly and has been very inconvenient in my life. I didn't take possession of the flat until July 2003 and even now I still haven't moved in completely. This is because the flats are not completely finished and are still having work done on them.

'I currently take a very mild anti-depressant and have taken this for about six years. I actually take less than the recommended dosage. I have also been prescribed Valium by my GP but have never used it.'

'I don't really tell my family everything about what I am thinking or feeling, because I don't think that they want to hear. I don't want to burden anyone or expose myself. I am a better listener and would rather listen to other people's worries. I have not changed my daily routine in any way and do not do things like lock my bedroom door at night. I am a little claustrophobic and would not be happy doing this.

'I still go out quite a lot but wouldn't come back late, especially alone. I always used to do things like get the last train home from London. I have been offered counselling, but I don't like that sort of thing. I considered it and dismissed it, as I don't think it would assist me. I consider the last 12 months as the most turbulent of my life. Time still doesn't erase the memory of what happened.'

Nor did it erase the recollections of Mrs K, then 78, who was burgled in March 2003 at her end-of-terrace home in West Dulwich. She had lived in the council-owned home for almost 40 years since she and her husband moved in and after his death in 1995 she had been there alone. Earlier in the year, she had been diagnosed with a slipped disc. Her statement was now delivered by the prosecuting counsel.

The day had begun as normal for Mrs K, with a yoghurt and banana for breakfast. Then, at around noon, after putting her 'smalls' in to soak, she had a lunch of a jacket potato, a slice of ham and a cup of tea. Later, she watched a *Midsomer Murders* episode on television and then, just before she went to bed in her blue-and-pink, flower-pattern nightdress, she put her tumble-drier on, as the electricity it used was cheaper at night.

The widow woke up at 2am – she could tell the time by the large wall clock in her room. She noticed that her rechargeable torch battery light was not flicking as it normally did, nor was the telephone light on.

'I must have sensed something as I turned to my left and there was this huge black figure and I thought, "How did he get in?" and the next thing he pushed me to the ground.' She kept a walking stick by her bed but 'this man was then on top of me and he put his hand over my mouth. I tried to fight with him. I was not able to move my stick but I grabbed him with my hand.' However, because the fabric of his clothes was slippery, she could not hold on to him. 'I had two or three goes but I could not hold on to it. I was feeling apprehensive and it did run through my mind that I was going to be attacked sexually.'

Yet again, in the dark of night in an elderly person's bedroom, came the dialogue that had been heard so often before:

'What do you want?'

'I want your money. Where's your money?'

Mrs K said, 'I told him I had not got any money. The only money is in my handbag by the table. There was not much in there, £10.' He tipped the handbag upside down and emptied all the contents out. She was still lying on the floor and estimated that she had been in that position for about 15 minutes. 'I just had to get up. I said, "Can you help me up please?"' The man came across to her and lifted her up 'in one movement'. The victim needed to sit in a chair and 'he was considerate in the way he got me up and helped me'.

The intruder now started to look around upstairs while his victim was downstairs. 'I did consider going to the front door but I did not think I could negotiate the front door and the step and then get to the gate before he came down.'

At one stage, he shone his trademark torch at some plates she had affixed to the wall. 'I said, "You can take them if you want" but he didn't.'

Then he got a damp cloth and wiped around her fingernails with it. She pleaded with him, 'Don't take my ring – I've had it for 50 years.' He said nothing in reply, but at least he didn't take it. She discovered later, however, that he had taken her 1945 engagement ring with five tiny diamonds in it, a gold ring and other pieces of jewellery. He'd also taken two £5 notes from inside a bag.

Eventually, he left and Mrs K put on the loose kaftan she often wore about the house and discovered the telephones had been disconnected. With blood down one side of her face, she went to a neighbour's home and said in a wavering voice, 'I have just been robbed and assaulted.' Family and friends, as well as the emergency services, were alerted. When the ambulance men reached her home, they found her sitting in a chair shaking.

'It wasn't until everyone had gone that the shock set in. I had a panic attack.'

The after-effects on his next victim, Mrs L, were even more pronounced. On 8 September 2004, Mrs L's three-bedroom semi-detached house in Bromley, Kent, had been the Stalker's next target. Her testimony was the second to be seen by the jury via a video recording. The hushed courtroom at Woolwich listened intently to every word the white-haired woman said as her description of her night of horror began.

Wearing a pink cardigan that she clutched tightly around her body, the 84-year-old widow told questioning officers that she heard 'a lot of clicking' the night of the attack, but thought that it was simply her windows rattling in the wind. It was about 1am.

An hour later, her ordeal was to begin. She heard a voice say, 'Don't scream. Don't scream. Where's the money?' in a quiet voice. She replied, '"Don't hurt me!" I was so frightened I did not know what to do.

'He did not push me about, which is a blessing ... but I could not stop shaking.'

Sometime after 3am, she remembers that the intruder was talking to her in a soft voice and urging her not to scream, his head close to hers as he said it. She used the word to describe that closeness as 'snuggled' – a word normally used in an affectionate, endearing way, but here it had a very strong undertone of menace.

Continually, he kept asking her, like an old-fashioned record that had become stuck in its groove, where the money was. Time after time, he would say it: 'Where's the money? Where's the money?'

At one stage, she had to go to the toilet. He stood in the doorway of the bathroom while she used it. 'As I came out of the door, he pushed me.' Her arm collided with the bathroom door. It was grazed and started to bleed and so they went downstairs to look for a plaster. He followed her as though attached to her. 'He was not letting me out of his sight.'

Still he kept on with the same, monotonous questioning. Where was the money? Where would he find money? She got the plasters out of a cupboard below the microwave and some scissors with which to cut it. He let her do so – he was not afraid. He didn't have anything to fear, did he? He was hardly likely to be attacked by an 84-year-old woman, no matter what she held in her hands.

Eventually, Mrs L told him, 'There is money in the drawer, tucked under the linen and the tea-towels.' It was £1,000 in a big, beige wallet, secured with a clip, that she had saved from her pension for new windows.

He took it – and then he was gone.

Mrs L contacted neighbours and told them of the attack. It was 3.18am and within minutes the police were on the scene.

Throughout the story of the Night Stalker, we have heard from the victims of his attacks, not just about the events of the night he came into their lives, but how it affected them subsequently. It also, of course, affected their loved ones. Perhaps Mrs L's son summarised the situation for many of their children, men and women who, because of the age of the victims, were middle-aged themselves.

He said, 'I am going to talk about how this offence has affected my mum's life. I am an only child and have no siblings. Prior to this incident, I would say my mum was a very independent lady. She used to do her own shopping, visit the bank, and collect her pension all by herself. She now does her shopping with a neighbour and also organises bank visits with her neighbour. She also has her pension paid directly into her bank account. I think the reason for this is that it gives her a sense of security and protection when she is carrying money with her.

'My mum has always enjoyed the garden. She would often go out there to feed the birds and squirrels and found it very peaceful. She would often lay in the garden and doze off. Since the incident, we have had to put up a fence, side gate and locks. It is more of an exercise yard as opposed to a garden. Before the incident, she used to potter around the front garden; now she will not go out there unless accompanied. She avoids going out there by herself.

'I would also like to say that my mum was in the throes of giving up smoking before the incident. She had cut it down to about a couple a day. Since the incident she has started smoking again; she is back to smoking 20 cigarettes a day.

'Almost on a daily basis when it gets to about twilight, she starts to lock the house up. She starts to draw the curtains, locks all the doors because she is so frightened. She will answer the door during the day if she knows who they are and if she is expecting them. She never answers the doors in the evening. To the best of my knowledge she also sets the alarm of an evening, certainly before she goes to bed, to give her added protection.

'I would only describe it as being a prisoner locked in your home. The incident has made my mum very jittery and when the phone rings she leaps up, and is frightened to answer it. If I am there, my mum expects me to answer the phone.'

A GP who saw the victim the day after the attack said, 'Prior to the break-in, Mrs L's physical health was good.

Her mental health was also good. However, she has always been a nervous person.

'She attended the surgery and saw the nurse. She stated that she had had a break-in and was attacked which resulted in a cut to her left forearm. This cut was dressed by the nurse. It did not require stitches, but had to be glued together. I was asked to see her while she was with the nurse and could see that she was very distressed and anxious and was visibly shaking, and stated that she was not sleeping very well. I prescribed her Temazepam. She attended the surgery the following day, 9 September 2004, to have her dressing changed.'

Some five and a half years later, the doctor added, 'I more recently saw her on Monday, 25 January 2010. The reason for the visit was because she was not sleeping due to the fact that the Night Stalker, as she refers to him, was soon to be at court. Physically, she was shaking and was very distressed and anxious. The incident was again coming back to her as a constant reminder of what had happened.'

The summer of 2009 had seen the spate of offences that led to the stepping-up of the hunt for the Stalker. On 25 May came that rarest of cases where Delroy Grant was concerned: an offence committed at a home where two people lived, not just one. It is impossible to say why he changed his modus operandi; perhaps the answer is the simplest one – he made a mistake.

The three-bedroom, semi-detached home in Bromley was occupied by a 62-year-old man, Mr M, and his elderly mother, who suffered from dementia. She had lived in the home for over 50 years, and he had lived with her since his divorce.

Before going to bed about 10pm that Sunday, Mr M's statement said, he had taken a carton of Tesco orange juice out of the fridge but had not opened it.

Later in the night, he noticed that his bedroom door was open and when he went out to investigate found a shoe, normally kept in a box-room, in the hall. He checked to make sure that his mother was all right and then went downstairs to discover he had been burgled. His jacket was on the floor, £30 was missing, all the doors and drawers were open and his mother's handbag had been turned upside down and its contents scattered; her bank cards lay all over the floor.

The burglar had entered through a kitchen window and the tool marks found around the window linked the break-in with similar offences in the area. Also, some of the orange juice had been drunk, leaving traces of the burglar's DNA on the carton.

On 6 June, the Stalker had struck again when he burgled the home of an 82-year-old dementia sufferer in South Croydon. Mrs N awoke to find a man going through her bedroom drawers. Because of her condition, she was unable to provide much information when questioned about the incident – she said she was sorry she could not remember more. The only description she could provide in her statement was that 'it was a man' who broke into her home. He did not assault her, she said, and had left.

Some might think this lady escaped lightly in comparison to other victims of the Stalker, but his visit still left its mark on her and her family. Her daughter spelled out the impact: 'My mother is 83 years old and she lives alone. She suffers from Alzheimer's disease and has done so the last four or so years.

'My mum has lived there for the past 50 years and was a teacher before she retired from working at a secondary school in Croydon. Her and my father were very active; he was eight years older than her. When Dad was 55 years old, he had a heart attack. They were both still quite active, though. They went folk-dancing several times a week. They enjoyed stamp collecting. Mum was learning the Greek language and had many friends who she would always go out with and many interests. Dad died 11 years ago at the age of 80; it was a big shock to her but her friends brought her through. She carried on with her life though and took up organ-playing. She felt very safe in her house; she'd brought up her children there and was very secure there.

'As a family, I think we noticed that Mum was getting forgetful, which gave us cause for concern. Also, a close neighbour had become concerned that Mum seemed different and had mentioned it to her doctor (they had the same doctor). Mum's GP arranged the brain scan. My sister went with Mum to the Maudsley Hospital for the scan, which revealed that Mum had Alzheimer's. This was December about four years ago. It was a big shock and I spent a lot of time with my mother over the following few weeks.

'She was prescribed Aricept (Donepezib) which slows down the process of dementia, and placed under the care of the Croydon Memory Service. She gradually gave up a few of her interests, like learning Greek, and cut down on some of her social life.

'We contacted Age Concern regarding getting a housekeeper and we got a lady who works every Wednesday for two hours at Mum's house ... We met with a company and arranged for someone to assist my mother every evening with the following things: taking her medication, cooking a meal and doing safety checks, for example, making sure the oven or other appliances hadn't been left on and checking window and door locks before leaving. A carer from Marion Homecare also comes in three lunchtimes a week to cook her lunch. This home-help service is paid for by us, the family. Apart from that, she has various other people that pop in for chats and I usually do her shopping every week and cook her lunch when I'm there.

'On the morning directly after the incident in June 2009, Mum called me at 7am and she was in a panic. I knew once she mentioned that her kitchen window was out and that the kitchen was cold that something had definitely happened. I got to her house in about half an hour ... Mum was very shaken up. The police said Mum had to go to the clinic, which we did. She complied with everything without complaint.

'I then brought Mum back to my house and she stayed with me for a few days. For Mum to be able to go back into her house, my brother-in-law had to make arrangements for Marion Homecare to provide someone to stay overnight with Mum every weekday for four to six weeks, while we – my sister, her husband and I – took it in turns to stay over at the weekends. The home-care person staying overnight cost extra and we had to rearrange our family commitments to stay at the weekends. This is because we were worried Mum would not settle in her house after the shock of someone breaking in.

'Mum did not feel secure in her home any more. Getting the windows fixed and changing the locks on the doors cost £701.50. It took five weeks for the windows to be fixed as the frame had to be made specially. Mum was very confused, anxious and insecure when she got back into her house. It took her between four to six weeks to really settle back, at which time we stopped the overnight cover.

'Mum has been having a regular yearly check-up to see how the Alzheimer's is progressing. Up until last year, when assessed, the Alzheimer's had been slowly progressing by a point each year. When Mum went for assessment in September/October 2009, three to four months after the incident, Mum's Alzheimer's had progressed by four points. This surprised the doctors and they asked had anything significant happened recently. The only significant event to have happened was the burglary. They were therefore told [of it]. The clinic now want to see her every six months as opposed to every year.

'Alzheimer's is a progressive disease, I know, but I feel that it is extremely likely that the shock of the break-in has accelerated the progress of the condition as she is now much less secure, less enthusiastic about the things she used to enjoy, more anxious and confused and less able to cope in her own home.'

'It's upsetting that [the Stalker] committed these crimes against the most vulnerable members of society. Having tried hard to keep her within an environment with which she is familiar, where she has lived for 50 years, it's upsetting that someone can, in one night, undermine our efforts and her confidence. A straightforward burglary would have been easier to understand, but I am very upset for Mum and the others affected by this man. I would like to see him locked away from society as he has obviously caused upset to a lot of elderly people, their families, friends and carers over a long period of time. I wish he'd been caught before but I'm glad that he's been locked away now and can't harm anyone else.

'The break-in and its aftermath was distressing to my mother, myself and everyone close to my mother. I have found talking about the incident and its aftermath quite upsetting.'

It was known that the Stalker's depravity involved both women and men, and this was brought home when one of his male victims spoke about the attack he had suffered. In the third video recording to be played in court, the jury heard 88-year-old Mr O, a grey-haired man wearing a white shirt and a black sleeveless cardigan, tell of the trauma he had suffered at his semi-detached home in Thornton Heath on the night of 13 August 2009.

'I was debating whether to have a bath or not,' he said. 'I had the radio on and I heard a noise like a bang. I thought this might have come from the radio.'

Mr O checked the dining-room window and then the kitchen windows, and then he went out on to the landing and saw a dark figure climbing the stairs. 'If I had phoned the police straight away [after hearing the noise], he might have been caught. But I spent so much time looking at windows that it allowed him to enter the house.'

The victim had been burgled in the recent past and he mistakenly thought it was the same man. 'I said, "Hello, we meet again."' The Stalker took him into a bedroom and indicated that his victim should undress. He helped him take off his clothes, everything apart from his socks. 'I thought he was going to murder me. I was praying to go for a quick death.'

Then the Stalker put his arms around the man's shoulders and began to fondle him intimately. 'That's when I realised that he was homosexual,' Mr O said. This went on for some time and the Stalker asked him at one stage, 'Are you scared? Are you nervous?' Then he allowed the old man, still only wearing his socks, to get up and pushed him towards the bathroom. The raider used the toilet and then allowed his hostage to go downstairs, by which time he had managed to put some clothing on.

Mr O couldn't remember whether he was asked for money or not, but the elderly man offered some anyway. He only had £15 and he gave it to him only to be told, '"No, I want more than that. I know you have more than that." I thought he was going to hit me. I was scared.'

Mr O reached for his grey backpack nearby and managed to find two £10 notes and four £5 notes in his purse. The burglar took the man's debit card, not credit card, and asked for the PIN number. Then he started looking through the man's documents and papers. 'I got the impression he was looking for money. He went through the top three drawers in great detail. In my top drawer on the left, he found a paperknife. He put it on the shelf.'

The man's ordeal was nearing an end. 'I could not see him smile but I had the feeling he smiled and he touched me on the shoulder as if to say, "We are still good friends." Asked about the man's voice, he said, 'It was a pleasant voice.'

Soon after the intruder fled, there was an unsuccessful attempt to use Mr O's debit card at 3.13am at a Lloyds TSB cashpoint in Lordship Lane, East Dulwich then two more unsuccessful attempts at a different cashpoint in Honor Oak Park 41 minutes later.

On 18 October, it had been the turn of an 87-year-old widow, Mrs P, to be a victim in her end-of-terrace home in Forest Hill. In her statement, she said that she had prepared for bed at about 11pm by changing into her nightie, brushing her hair and saying her prayers.

Sometime between 2.30am and 2.45am, she awoke and crossed the landing to go to the toilet, after which she returned to her bedroom to sleep again.

The next thing she recalled was a 'knock' on the side of her head and she thought she might have hit something. She turned around and she saw a silhouette and there was a light shining in her eyes. The figure began to look into her bedside cabinets. 'I said to him, "I have not got anything here. I have had a few burglaries and I have nothing left."' She told him that all she had was some jewellery in the bottom drawer and he looked in it. She told him he could take a credit card that he had found.

He then pulled her bedclothes back and touched her around the top of her thigh before replacing the bedclothes. 'He seemed to take a long time over this, as though he had all the time in the world.' The Stalker then went out and then came back with his torch in hand, pulled her bedclothes down and beckoned her to follow. She replied, 'I can't walk that far, you know,' and he waited while she took her time to get out of bed and then put her dressing gown on.

He allowed her to get out of bed, holding her hand as she did so. She said to him, 'I can't stand very long, you know.' Nevertheless, he led her to another room on the first floor and sat her in a chair. He then opened some desk drawers and gave her a pen and paper. She didn't know why: did he want her to write something down? Did he want her to provide her name for him? He leaned down and whispered something in her ear. She could not hear it. Then he wrote something down. She could not read it without her glasses. Only then did she realise that he wanted the PIN number of her bank card. She gave it to him. 'If I gave him the wrong number, he might come back and take his revenge on me,' she explained.

After she had given it to him, she sat on her futon for about five minutes. She then looked around the house and saw that the back door was open. He had left. It was 5.40am and he had gone from her life as silently as he had entered it.

The Stalker had returned to his favourite type of target for his next known attack: a two-bedroom chalet-style bungalow. It was in Shirley and its occupant was a recently widowed 82-year-old who had lived there for almost 60 years. The woman, known as Mrs Q, had been a nurse in a hospital in Chelsea before ceasing work to look after her daughter and husband.

Intriguingly, her home was very near the one that featured in the aborted raid in mid-November that led to the Stalker's arrest. In addition, there was a sighting of a Vauxhall Zafira at 3.36am on a CCTV camera near her home – the car that police believe the burglar used that night.

Mrs Q was burgled on the night of 29 October. 'I was woken by the sound of a male voice,' she said in her statement. 'He said, "Where's your money?" I said I had not got any.' She told him more than six times she had no money. He left the room and she later discovered that her handbag with £200 in it was missing.

Fortunately for this old lady, there was no attack on her and her encounter with the Stalker was, by the standards of some of his other victims, minimal. Nevertheless, it had an impact on her that cannot be lightly dismissed – an illustration, if one was needed, of the havoc that the Stalker could cause the innocent.

'I have had a very happy life. I have been extremely happy and very lucky. The neighbours have always been very helpful. I am still very active and get out a lot. I always walk to the library.

'My home is a semi-detached two-bedroom chalet bungalow. The two bedrooms upstairs are quite large, and I have a living room and dining room at the front, either side of the front door. The hall extends down the middle towards the stairs. At the rear of the property downstairs, there is a kitchen, and a bathroom and toilet combined. There is another room at the rear that overlooks the back garden.

'Since my husband died, I have been using that as a bedroom. It saves me from going up and down the stairs during the night to use the toilet. The staircase has a couple of nasty turns and can be quite awkward. The only door apart from the front door is one that leads out from the kitchen into the garden.

'I have a bit of routine at nights. I normally go to bed about 10pm, unless there's something very good on the television. I watch the television or read a book in the front living room. Whilst watching the television I have the front curtains closed, with the lights on. However, when I go to bed I turn off the lights and then open up the curtains fully. When I go into the bedroom I'm using, the curtains are open. However, I close them when I get undressed. I then open them before getting into bed. In essence, once I'm in bed all the curtains in the house are open.

'So that's as it was on 28 October 2009. I was in bed by 10pm to 10.30pm. I fell asleep easily as I normally do. The twin beds in the room are behind and to the right hand side of the door as you enter. I was sleeping in the bed nearest the door. I always leave the door open. All the other doors in the house are locked. I had my handbag as normal beside the left side of the bed and slightly under the bed.

'I was woken by the sound of a male voice. He was stood to my left. He said, "Where's your money?" That's all he said. He kept repeating the same words. "Where's your money?" Each time he said it, I responded by saying, "I haven't got any." I estimate he repeated these words six to eight times. His voice wasn't threatening – it was just monotonous. His voice was at normal tone. It didn't make me feel frightened. I wonder now if he thought there may be someone else upstairs. He had an English accent. I think he was beside me for a few minutes only. Then it went quiet and he disappeared.

'My immediate reaction was to get out of bed straight away and go to the telephone in the hall. I did that and dialled 999. I was put through to the police. I was on the phone within a minute or so of him leaving. At no time did the man touch me. All I can say is that there was a man next to me. I cannot describe him in any way. It was just a male voice. I know now that my handbag was stolen from beside the bed. But I didn't know that till much later.

'The police arrived and I told them what happened. I was asked if I wanted to go to hospital but I didn't want to go. My neighbour across the road came over. He then took me back to his house. I was only dressed in a nightie, dressing gown and slippers.

'I subsequently learned that [the intruder] came through a window. The handbag was never found. It contained about £200 cash, plus an Alliance and Leicester-related bank card. That was cancelled by my son-in-law. The rest was normal items: pens, purse with loose change, keys to my home. I have had the locks changed. I can't now think of anything else.

'In fact, since the burglary, my memory has deteriorated considerably. It has left me feeling a bit vulnerable and on edge. I now want to leave the house I have loved so much. It can never be the same. In the New Year, I plan to sell the house, and move down to Devon. It is a shame to leave the home I have had so many happy times and such lovely memories. Since the burglary, I don't love the house the way I did. I can't wait to get out and go down to Devon. I feel so alone now. I did not give anyone permission to enter my home and steal any of my possessions. I would not admit to it before, but since the incident I feel like an old lady. Before I didn't.'

There is a common thread through all the victims' stories, be they told in a written fashion to police soon after the burglary or physical assault, recorded during questioning, or in the form of impact statements made some time later in which they assessed how much the crime had affected them.

Everyone, men and women, suffered from the Stalker's entry into their lives and homes. They all valued the comfort that living in their own bungalows or small houses gave them – that sense of homeliness, tranquillity and security it gave them. After Delroy Grant arrived in the middle of the night to torment them, none of them was ever the same again.

CHAPTER THIRTEEN

Delroy Grant's trial was making headlines around the world. A succession of police witnesses and experts were called for the prosecution to continue the case against him.

Det. Con. Steven Purvis spoke of the remark Grant made to him while having his fingerprints taken on the Sunday of his arrest at 2.55pm. 'I explained to him that he should relax and let me do all the work,' he told the court. 'During the course of taking the prints, I said, "I'm making sure I am getting ink all over your hands and get a good print from them." He replied, "I don't know why you are bothering. I always wear gloves."' The officer testified that he had made no further comment and carried on taking the fingerprints, moving from right to left on the inked brass plate he used, but made a note of them at 4pm once he had finished clearing up.

Det. Con. Purvis now faced questioning by the man who had the task of defending Grant, Courtenay Griffiths QC.

Mr Griffiths was one of the country's leading barristers. He had been involved in many high-profile cases in the preceding quarter of a century, including defending (while still a junior lawyer) the IRA members accused of involvement in the Harrods and Brighton bombings. He had also worked on the London Docklands bombing case in 1996, Winston Silcott's trial for the murder of PC Keith Blakelock and the first trial relating to the death of Damilola Taylor, the ten-year old schoolboy who had died in an incident in Peckham. Mr Griffiths was also appearing for the former President of Liberia Charles Taylor in the extended and high-profile 'blood diamonds' trial in the Hague; one newspaper had recently commented: 'Forget Naomi Campbell, the real star of the Taylor trial is Griffiths QC.' A Facebook fan page had subsequently been set up in honour of the Jamaican-born barrister.

Mr Griffiths put it to the officer that there had been a general conversation going on at the time of the fingerprinting. 'He said, in a rather light-hearted way, that if he was going to commit a burglary "I would put gloves on."'

Mr Purvis replied, 'That's incorrect, your Honour.'

The court also heard from Det. Con. Joanne Crockford, an officer who had been part of the Minstead team for seven years. On 19 November, she had gone to see Grant. 'I went to his cell and told him that he was going to court early that morning and I would not be attending. He was quite agitated and he was pacing his cell and I asked him was anything wrong.

'He said, "I do not want to fit anyone up."

'I asked him what did he mean, and he replied, "Have you thought about my son?"'

The officer asked him which son he was referring to – she knew he had several – and he replied, 'Delroy Junior.' She then asked him why he thought Delroy Junior could have been responsible for any of the crimes that had been discussed by police and the man they had arrested, and he said, 'He lives in the right area and he is the same height as me.' The detective told him she would have to pass the information on and he said, 'No, don't pass it on. I don't want to fit anyone up.'

Mr Kevin Majid, a civilian officer who worked for the custody office at Lewisham police station, told the court that at about 7.30am he went to cell 1c where Grant was being held. Grant had buzzed for attention and, when Mr Majid got there, Grant said he wanted to speak to his solicitor. Mr Majid said he would pass on the request but then 'Mr Grant then said words to the effect that he would admit everything now. He said he would admit it rather than be stuck in a cell for three days [waiting his next court appearance].'

The court also was told of the full list of what had been found in the Vauxhall Zafira after Grant's arrest. In it were no less than 46 exhibits, including a dark-blue cagoule jacket in the front of the vehicle, a black zipper jacket, a pair of brown slip-on shoes, a black woolly hat, a flat cap, a grey zip fleece and a light grey Nike beanie cap. In the boot, there were a pair of black patent shoes, a pair of metal pincers or pliers, a claw hammer, a crowbar or case-opener, a grey sock in the driver's door pocket. Also in the car were a pair of metal grips, like pliers, with a blue handle.

Expert witnesses were called, including Mr Raymond Chapman, a forensic scientist, who explained how DNA profiling worked and its history. During a lengthy spell in the witness box, Mr Chapman also gave details of the similarities between the DNA samples found at the Stalker's crime scenes – and on items found in the car – and that of Delroy Grant. In most cases, the chances of it being anyone other than Grant's DNA were a billion to one, the highest statistical level the process went up to. Mr Chapman further said that, after Grant's arrest, samples were taken from his family and associates and they could be ruled out of the crime-scene DNA. He also pointed out the difficulty of keeping body fluid samples for a long period of time and then obtaining an exact result from them.

If the evidence that the court had heard so far was compelling, it was nothing compared with what was to come. On the morning of 16 March, Delroy Grant's first wife, Janet Watson, stepped into the witness box and gave her remarkable rebuttal to one of the strangest defences ever heard before an English court.

Janet Watson had already spoken briefly about her life

with Delroy Grant in interviews at the time of his arrest and told of the kind of man he was. The prosecuting counsel, Mr Laidlaw, had already outlined to the jury that Grant's defence to the charges was that his first wife had kept his body fluids from the late 1970s and they had subsequently been planted at the scene of his crimes. Her reaction to the questions that were put to her was spellbinding.

The London-born woman, wearing a colourful top and with her hair in long braids, was told by Mr Laidlaw when she entered the witness box, 'Quite serious allegations have been made against you and I would like you to hear those.'

Janet gave some brief biographical description before going into detail about her life with Grant. Her daughter Shirley had been born when Janet was 17 but she had split up with the child's father. In the mid-1970s, when she was 17 or 18 and was living in Bermondsey, she went to a local pub, leaving her infant daughter in the corridor of the pub (presumably in a pram or pushchair). Then she noticed that Grant was talking to the youngster and she told him not to. But then they got talking.

'He was really nice, fantastic. He was a charmer. He was very softly spoken, really, really nice.' She emphasised the second 'really', drawing the word out for as long as she could, as if to emphasise the spell that he had put over her. 'We just seemed to click. We went out the next evening and the next week he moved in.' At the end of that week, he had proposed and she had accepted.

'To me, I had found my Prince Charming.' In October 1975, just two or three months after that first meeting, they married at St Laurence Church, Bromley.

Mr Laidlaw put it to her: 'Things between the two of you turned really sour, did they not?'

'Well sour,' she replied. It was only a matter of weeks before it became clear that the relationship could not continue. 'He made it obvious it was not going to be a nice time,' she said. Although the relationship was, in her words 'very painful', they had two sons, Delroy Junior in February 1976 and Michael in October 1978. Nevertheless, the marriage was not a happy one and by the time she was 22 she had filed for divorce.

She had then met another man and they married. 'It was a much better relationship. I was his princess and I was treated very well.' With a new husband she had a son who died aged 17 after suffering from sickle-cell disease.

Referring to Grant, she initially said that after they had separated in 1979 they did not have contact. 'I did not see him at all. It was beautiful.' She went on to say that about ten years later she had met him at school one day and he had asked if he could see his sons. They arranged for it to happen the next day but, she said, he did not turn up. She did not know what had happened to him. 'I did not want to see him again.'

The court had already heard scientific evidence explaining that in the 1970s – when Grant and Janet were together – the use of DNA to trace or eliminate suspects in criminal cases still lay years in the future. Mr Laidlaw now raised the matter of Grant's DNA with her. Some time after Grant's arrest, the police had come to her and said that Grant was making allegations about her. Mr Laidlaw asked what her reaction to these allegations – the planting of the DNA – was and she replied, 'I was speechless. I was amazed. It was unbelievable.'

At this point, Grant, who had remained fairly emotionless throughout his trial so far, shouted out, 'You are a liar!'

Mr Laidlaw continued by spelling out the claim that between 1975 and 1979 she had collected his semen.

'It's ridiculous,' she said. 'I did not.' She said that during their marriage she was on the pill and Grant did not use a condom. 'I had no understanding of DNA,' she said. 'I have no knowledge of that.'

The prosecutor asked if she knew how to store body fluids.

'To this day I don't know,' she replied.

Asked about having a white associate who might help her she was adamant: 'There's no truth in that whatsoever. No, there is no truth.'

Under cross-examination by Mr Griffiths, for Grant, Janet gave more details of her early life with the accused man. After that first meeting, they had gone on a date the following evening to the Charlie Chaplin pub in the Elephant and Castle. Soon after their marriage, Grant was involved with a music system business called Sir Cosmic Sound. Later, he worked for a builders' merchant, but then he got into trouble with the police and was jailed.

Mr Griffiths put it to her: 'The relationship from shortly after it started had great difficulties, did it not?'

'It had very great difficulties,' she admitted, adding that he was violent to her and agreeing he was a 'serious womaniser'.

Mr Griffiths said, 'You began to hate him, didn't you?'

'I was not fond of him,' she replied.

Mr Griffiths now put it to her that she was concerned that Grant might transfer a sexual disease to her, and that she had a friend at Guy's Hospital who could find out if this was the case, so she decided to get a sample of her husband's body fluids.

'I am sorry, you are wrong,' she said.

Mr Griffiths then put to her the suggestion that this friend at Guy's gave her several bottles and she had Grant masturbate into them, and then gave the bottles containing the semen to this friend.

'None of this is true,' she replied. 'I think his imagination is getting the best of him.'

'I am suggesting that you, with a white male accomplice, planted Delroy's samples around various burglaries in south east London,' Mr Griffiths insisted.

'I did not have a white accomplice,' she retorted. 'I don't go out with white men. I don't know anyone. ... I am in no campaign against him whatsoever. ... I left him. ... I don't know what he is talking about. He needs help.'

Mr Griffiths continued by putting it to her that Grant said she was a liar.

'And I say he is a storyteller,' was her reply.

'He says that you have set him up for these offences.'

'I don't know what is wrong with him.'

Six months prior to his arrest, she added, Grant's sons had wanted to look him up, so she went with them to visit him but stayed in the car. He came out to her. 'He was shaking my hand and started telling me his stories. I was only polite to him because my son asked me to be.'

Her evidence over, the prosecution case came to an end. The defence was now to have its turn, and at 3.15pm that day came the event the court had been waiting for: Mr Griffiths told the judge, 'My Lord, I call Delroy Grant.'

With a prison warder on either side of him, the pin-stripe-suited, bespectacled Grant made his way from the confines of the dock and its security screen to the witness box. He affirmed that his evidence would be true rather than swearing on the Bible and, in response to his barrister's questioning, gave some details of his early years.

As we already know, he came from Jamaica to join his father in London when he was in his early teens. Asked about life with his father and stepmother, Grant said, 'Life was all right, but I found my parents restrictive. They were good parents but fairly strict. That's the way we were brought up in Jamaica.'

Talking of his meeting with his wife-to-be Janet, he said that they did not meet initially at a pub; rather it was when she came into the garage where he worked. The couple married and for a spell her brother lived with them until he went to America. He was heavily involved with

Sir Cosmic Sound, he said, adding, 'I liked to play music, I liked to go out to nightclubs.'

His favourite nightclub was the Bouncing Ball on Peckham High Street. There he had met a girl there called Glendeen and, after he'd finished a relationship with her, he'd started seeing a woman called Rosemary Burrell, who had four children and lived in Dulwich. Mr Griffiths put it to him: 'Would you accept this, Mr Grant – you were seriously unfaithful to your wife?'

'With reasons, yes,' he replied.

He explained this by adding that Janet had told him she had finished with the man who had fathered her child. 'After we got married, it was not the case. He was coming to the house by the time I was leaving the house in the morning, and he was leaving when I was coming home at night. ... I and Janet would fight like cats and dogs.'

Grant had then taken part in a raid on a post office in Dulwich which resulted in his being jailed, and it was while he was in prison that she had divorced him. 'Janet was bitter towards me because of the relationships I had and the violence I inflicted on her sometimes.'

Grant then went on to recount his complicated love life. By the time he was 20 or 21 he was living with Rosemary Burrell – 'who was quite older than I was' and she had a daughter Samantha by him. After prison, he went to live with her and she moved to Herne Hill. He was there for about one and half years, until he met a woman called June Finley from Leicestershire, which resulted in him eventually moving there. Then, in 1991, he married Jennifer. 'I met Jennifer when I was with June,' he said, but, although he married Jennifer, he continued to see June. 'For a while, I was seeing these two women at the same time. It caused friction and they fought.'

Sadly, Jennifer developed multiple sclerosis and by 2003 he was her principal carer. The next year he became her full-time carer.

In answer to questioning by Mr Griffiths, Grant said that he had ten children – eight he fathered himself and two he 'inherited'. He had two sons with Janet, his first wife, and two sons with Jennifer, his second. There was also the daughter by Rosemary and three sons with June. In addition, Jennifer had two daughters from another relationship.

Grant also told of a woman called Barbara Stocks who, he said, was 'a very close friend' and with whom he began a relationship in 2003. That relationship was ongoing at the time of his arrest.

He agreed with his counsel that there was no dispute over the fact that the offences listed in court had been committed. He was saying, however, that he was not responsible for them. 'The DNA was planted by someone else … Janet Watson with someone else,' he told the court. Asked who that other person might be, he replied, 'Unknown person at this time.'

When Janet found out about his relationship with another woman, Grant said, she refused to sleep with him. 'She was not going to have sex with me because she was concerned that I had caught something. She said the only way that can take place is if I have my saliva and semen tested and she knew someone who could do that who worked at Guy's Hospital.' His then wife made him produce semen into six plastic cups and saliva into another cup, he said, which she then put into two bottles. It took him a week to complete his task, he told the court.

Mr Griffiths asked, 'After you provided these samples, what happened?'

Grant replied, 'On one occasion, someone on a motorbike pulled up downstairs and hooted the horn. Janet brought two bottles to this guy, who had a helmet on and a white coat.'

Mr Griffiths then raised a point with him. 'You accept that the semen samples observed by forensic scientists came from vaginal swabs? Can you help us as to how this unknown man was able to do that?'

Grant replied, 'By using instruments – I assume a syringe.'

Mr Griffiths pointed out that, if the samples had been taken in 1977, it would be another 15 years before they were 'placed' at the scene of a crime, and this would then continue over a further 17-year period.

When asked what motivated her and why she would wait 15 years to start her campaign, Grant said, 'Malice, hatred, violence maybe – all the problems in our relationship. I can't think of any reason she waited 15 years.'

On the day of his arrest, Grant said, he had been with Barbara Stocks earlier and then had arranged to go and collect some cannabis. He went to an area of Gypsy Hill to begin with but the person he had arranged to meet did not show up. He then got a call from the man and went to a new rendezvous point, this time in Shirley, an area he had been to several times in the preceding three months. At about 10.30pm, he got a call from the dealer who said he had been held up. Eventually, Grant left and drove off. 'I decided I was not going to do this any more, wait for a dealer to come to me, so I left in a huff.'

Later, he saw a car behind him. He thought it might be his dealer so he drove slowly, but when the car got close to him it put on a flashing blue light and pulled up alongside. He knew then it was the police.

Earlier in the case, the jury had been told that Grant had given incorrect names initially and also that a torch had been found on him. In his evidence, however, Grant denied this and said the officers had been lying.

He was wearing two pairs of jeans, three tops and two underpants. Mr Griffiths asked him about the clothing and why would he wear two sets of underpants.

'This is a common thing,' Grant replied, 'wearing two underpants. I wear boxer shorts and a tighter pair below to hold myself in place. I don't like to hang around.' The two pairs of jeans were because he had been working that day at Barbara Stocks' and he wore one on top for protection and, he insisted, they had paint on them to illustrate his point. And the three tops? 'I normally wear two T-shirts anyway and I was wearing the shirt because I was decorating.'

Grant further testified that his remark about

fingerprints and gloves at the station was 'said in jest' and that he never said anything later on about admitting the offences. The man who said he did, Mr Majid, was a liar, he said. Nor did he recollect making any remark about the possibility of crime-scene DNA belonging to his son.

Questioned further about the fleece and crowbar found in the Zafira after he was stopped, he said, 'I believe both the fleece and the crowbar were planted by an accomplice of Janet Watson.'

Mr Griffiths continued by asking about a glove found near one of the crime scenes that contained DNA belonging to him and Barbara Stocks. 'I believe that the DNA was planted in the glove and taken to the scene of the crime and left nearby,' was his answer. The glove, he claimed, could have been taken from her bin. The torches in the car were explained away with the answer, 'Because we normally go camping and I use a lot of torches for my decorating.'

Prosecutor Jonathan Laidlaw QC wasted little time when it came to cross-examining Grant. 'Your defence that somebody planted your DNA is a lie born out of desperation, and also because you have a complete inability to face up to what you have done,' he said. 'The idea that Janet Watson was behind this elaborate scheme to frame you is pure fiction and fantasy ... an absolute invention by you from start to finish.'

Mr Laidlaw pressed the point by asking several times why Grant had not raised this defence when he was first arrested, and why was it only later that he mentioned it?

Why had Grant not said, 'Look, you ought to know that back in 1977 an ex-wife of mine had samples of my semen?'

'At the time I did not link the two together,' Grant said.

Mr Laidlaw continued, 'You did not have a genuine defence at all in November, just one that you have made up since.'

Then Grant hit back. 'For what reason would I want to rape old women?'

There was a moment's silence as the barrister's eyes met Grant's, and then Mr Laidlaw replied, 'That's a very good question. But I'm not allowed to answer questions, I ask the questions ... But it is a very good question.'

Mr Laidlaw said Grant would 'stoop to any level' to avoid prosecution and his defence was a 'complete fabrication from start to finish' but Grant denied the QC's statement that he had a 'complete inability' to face up to his crimes.

Mr Laidlaw then pressed Grant on his claim that Janet Watson had kept his semen for decades. 'If these charges were not so grave, this could be almost laughable as an account,' he said. 'The idea that Janet Watson, who has already suffered at your hands, was behind this elaborate scheme to frame you is pure fiction and fantasy – an elaborate invention by you from start to finish.'

When Mr Laidlaw said Ms Watson was a 'thoroughly decent hard-working mother', Grant said, 'I do not accept that.'

Mr Laidlaw added later, 'You are a liar who changes his position whenever it is necessary to do so.'

Grant replied, 'I change nothing.'

Grant said he could not say why Ms Watson would wait 15 years to commit the first crime or why she never reported his name to police in a bid to frame him. He believed the first bid to frame him was a 'prototype' as there was not another attack for six years.

He again said his decision to wear so many clothes was linked to the decorating work he was doing. But Mr Laidlaw said the outfit was a 'burglary kit' so he could quickly change appearance to avoid detection by CCTV cameras at cash machines.

Mr Laidlaw then began to dissect the DNA explanation that Grant had given to the court. He said that Grant had assumed that his son would have similar DNA to his own and that was why he mentioned the young man. Again, Mr Laidlaw pointed out that it had been 14 months between Grant's arrest and the emergence of his story that Janet Watson had stored and planted the DNA.

When Mr Laidlaw asked how many women Grant had slept with during his adult life, the reply came back: 'A few. ... maybe six, maybe more.'

'Is it about six, Mr Grant, or is it many more than that?' the barrister asked. He then continued by asking why, if there had been concern about having a sexually transmitted disease and passing it on all those years ago, he did not go to a doctor or a Sexually Transmitted Disease clinic.

Grant replied, 'I was the guilty party and so I submitted to her request.'

Why, asked Mr Laidlaw, did he simply not go to a doctor or clinic and get examined?

All Grant replied was that his ex-wife knew someone at Guy's Hospital, although he did not know who that person was.

Mr Laidlaw then raised the point of whether an answer ever came back from the hospital.

Grant said, 'I kept asking her when she would get the results and this went on for a couple of weeks. She said she had not heard and that's when I started getting annoyed.'

'Mrs Watson is not behind these offences at all,' Mr Laidlaw told him. 'You were her softly spoken charmer, as she described, but once you were married you treated her badly.'

Grant responded by saying that when they were married she had affairs.

Mr Laidlaw told him, 'She is a thoroughly decent, hard-working mother who has had nothing to do with trying to get you in trouble.'

After a short break, Mr Laidlaw continued to examine Grant's story. He referred to the attack on Mrs A and her subsequent rape. 'How was it the rapist was able to use a syringe to put semen inside Mrs A at the same time as he was squeezing her face?' he asked.

Grant replied, 'Because he has two hands, hasn't he? There's a possibility that she did not know it was a syringe not a penis. If she was being raped, would she know?'

Asked about the attack on Mrs G and again the

description that made it clear no syringe was used, Grant just said, 'I did not commit these crimes.'

Mr Laidlaw said, 'It's not a case of you refusing to face up to what you have done, is it?'

'It's a fact,' replied Grant.

The prosecutor next referred to the victim who was kissed on the cheek and traces of Grant's DNA subsequently being taken from her face. 'How is it possible for the intruder to kiss her without leaving his own DNA but leaving yours?'

'There's a possibility that he knows how to kiss someone on the face without leaving his DNA and leaving mine,' was the reply.

Mr Laidlaw asked him if he was being serious.

'Yes,' Grant replied. 'It could have been done with a sponge.'

Mr Laidlaw then raised the point, that if Janet Watson had been responsible for the planting of DNA in 1992, why had she waited years before doing the same thing again? Why not just ring up the police after the first attack and say, 'The rapist you are looking for is Delroy Grant,' and put the phone down?

'I can't help you with that,' said Grant.

Mr Laidlaw then turned his attention to the glove found near the scene of one of the crimes and Grant's assertion that it could have been taken from Barbara Stocks' dustbin. 'You told the jury some cock-and-bull story about DNA being removed from Ms Stocks' bin. Utter, utter rubbish and you are a liar who changes his position when he wants to.'

Even as his evidence drew to a close, Grant insisted, 'I am not the Minstead offender.'

Mr Laidlaw had now to sum up for the Crown. He could not have put it more succinctly when he said, 'The nature of these offences – burglaries carried out at night by a highly skilled and proficient individual and then attacks launched upon the victims who were alone in their houses – really is the stuff of nightmares and what keeps us all awake at night.

'The deliberate targeting of the elderly takes the offending in this case to an altogether more serious level, and then there was the sickening and depraved nature of the sexual attacks suffered by nine of the victims. It was one thing to steal but then to launch gratuitous sexual attacks to humiliate was to take the offending to an altogether different scale. What could have motivated the perpetrator to commit offences such as these is difficult if not impossible to understand. Did he never stop to consider the impact of what he was doing to the elderly in the last years of their lives or think about their families? No, he did not.'

Mr Laidlaw went on to say that Grant's explanation that it was his ex-wife who had arranged for his DNA to be planted at the crimes was 'a quite extraordinary account which simply defies belief'.

'It's such an incredible account that to respond to it is almost to dignify it. He simply refuses to face up to what he has done. His arrogance is such he assumes we will accept literally anything he will say.'

In reference to Grant's evidence from the witness box, he asked the jury, 'Was the account true or was it clear to you that his was simply a performance, and not a very good one at that, in an attempt to deceive and mislead you?'

Referring to the DNA and other evidence and then the 'burglar's kit' in his car, he added, 'It's an absolutely compelling case against the defendant.'

Mr Laidlaw also drew attention to Grant's reference at the police station to his son and to the remark to Mr Majid that he might confess to everything. 'It's all desperate stuff. The behaviour of a man with nowhere to turn.

'You have seen the last roll of the dice: the "I've been framed by ex-wife defence". Is it possible, do you think, that Janet Watson, assisted by an unknown accomplice with a syringe, committed these offences in an attempt to frame this man?

'You have seen Janet Watson. You have seen her and the defendant. Who would you believe?' He also pointed out that in the evidence of the victims there had been no mention of a syringe, and how would it have been possible for any other man to carry out the crimes and not leave traces of his own DNA?

'Do you think it possible that the defendant was a victim of a plot to frame him? ... The explanation is that, so strong is the evidence against him, he is driven to run a defence which has the appearance of being absurd. What else could he say? When confronted with this barrage of evidence, you do have to come up with a defence which is as mad as this one.'

Referring to Janet Watson, Mr Laidlaw said, 'Did she look or sound to you like someone who could have done what the defendant said? ... She is an ordinary, thoroughly decent woman who has done nothing wrong. Her misfortune was to encounter this man and fall for him before his true colours were revealed.'

Pointing out that the man who pioneered DNA use in crime-solving, Professor Alec Jeffries, did not do so until the mid-1980s, he queried, 'Before the academics and scientists had thought of a way of recovering semen, Janet Watson was way ahead of all these people? How would she have been able to store and preserve it for all those years?'

And of the woman kissed on the cheek and where Grant's DNA was subsequently found, he said, 'Did he have a capsule in his mouth, James Bond-like, to project the defendant's DNA and conceal his own?'

The barrister continued to take Grant's story apart. How would Janet Watson have got hold of the glove belonging to Barbara Stocks? And, if she did, why did she leave it some distance from the house that was burgled?

'We suggest the defence played out for you is an act of desperation. He is prepared to do or say anything to avoid responsibility.'

Summing up for the defence, Courtenay Griffiths QC made no bones about the crimes committed against this series of elderly people. 'These truly are acts of real wickedness,' he said. 'There is something uniquely revolting about these offences. All rape is appalling – the rape and indecent assault of these elderly people is worse.' The crimes, he said, 'mesmerise and enrage us. They create a kind of revulsion.'

But, he pointed out, it was for the prosecution to prove its case, and added, 'What is required of you, members of the jury, is passionless reason.'

Judge Peter Rook QC took four hours to deliver his summary. In it, while acknowledging the horror of the crimes before them, he told the jury not to let their 'understandable disgust and revulsion' taint their deliberations.

He told the jury that the combination of the DNA evidence and the similarities between the 'nature and manner' of the offences meant the jury must be 'led to the sure conclusion it was one person' who committed all the crimes. In his conclusion, the judge pointed out that, if the jury found Grant guilty of one offence, they were obliged to find him guilty of all other counts.

At 3.05pm on Tuesday, 22 March, the jury was sent out to consider its verdict. There were those willing to put money on the fact that they would return before the court rose for the day, so strong was the evidence against Grant. But they didn't, nor did they return the next day either. It wasn't until the Thursday morning, when, shortly after 10am, the judge told them he was prepared to accept a majority verdict, one in which at least ten of them agreed, that the case came to an end.

At 10.36am, the 12 men and women returned to court

and the foreman of the jury began to deliver their verdicts. Grant, surrounded in the dock by three guards in crisply ironed white shirts, stood as impassive as ever as he was found guilty on all 29 counts by a majority of ten to two. It was not until 10.51am that the jury foreman finished his list.

The judge then excused the members of the jury from future service and said he would pass sentence the next day at 10am. Addressing counsel, he said, 'My own researches have revealed no case that is similar to this. ... The guidelines don't envisage this kind of case.'

Speaking to Grant, he said he would not pass sentence that day, as there were various matters that the barristers had to put before him, but 'the main sentence will be very long indeed'.

Grant said nothing. He looked as impassive as he had been for much of the case, almost disinterested. The only time he showed any emotion was when the judge referred to him as 'dangerous'. He just shook his head.

CHAPTER
FOURTEEN

Court number three was packed the next morning as Delroy Grant was brought from the cells to hear his sentence. Numerous officers linked with Operation Minstead, including Det. Supt. Simon Morgan who had been hunting the Stalker for years, were there. The public gallery was filled with relatives of victims who had suffered at Delroy Grant's hands.

Before sentence was passed, however, both prosecuting and defence counsel were to address the court again.

Jonathan Laidlaw QC began by saying it was not for a barrister to summarise the impact on the elderly of the Night Stalker's crimes, but he said, 'The sexual acts were to elevate the seriousness and the harm caused to a height seldom seen.' In a series of remarks drawn from the impact statements his victims had made, he went on to list the accounts of his victims and the consequences to their comfort and frame of mind in the ensuing years. The jury who had decided his guilt heard these for the first time.

There was the 89-year-old who 'could not live alone' after his attack and the 81-year-old who said, 'It's a nasty feeling knowing that a stranger has been through your home,' and added, 'I have to live with the fear that he will return.' There was the 71-year-old who, even ten years after being burgled, said, 'I do not sleep well out of fear that I will be attacked in my own home.' Then there was the 82-year-old, now dead, who had been raped and who'd said, 'I try to forget but I can't.'

Two women spoke to the court that morning too.

One was the daughter of the then 82-year old whose home in Addiscombe had been burgled and who had been subjected to an indecent assault by Grant. She had died in 2004, but two years before passing away she had told police, 'I never wanted to leave my home because of what happened. I was not going to move because of that wretched man.' Her daughter, who had been at court for most of the trial, was called to the witness box and told the court, 'She refused to be considered a victim. She was a very strong character but she thought about it every day of her life. She refused to be turned out of that house by that wretched man. She loved that house and had happy memories there and refused to leave it.'

Next to speak was the one victim of an attack who had appeared in court in person, and whose recollection was not purely captured on filmed footage or through written statements. She had not been required to give evidence as there was no dispute about what had happened to her, merely who the perpetrator had been.

Miss J was the woman who, at the age of 77 in October 2002, had been indecently assaulted by Grant at her home in Shirley. She began by saying to Mr Laidlaw, 'Could I say how much the statements we have heard resonate with me?' She listened intently as Mr Laidlaw read from her impact statement, nodding as he did so, and when he had finished she added, 'I just felt ... I don't know why he wanted to do these things.'

At this stage, the judge leaned forward and asked her whether time had helped to heal the effects on her. She replied, 'If I go out, I like to be home before dark and I do a lot of bolting and locking and taking precautions. It changed my life.'

Mr Laidlaw continued to read from the statements of the other victims and ended by saying this had been just a small selection of their remarks and that he hoped he had done justice to all the victims.

Mr Laidlaw also gave details of the police operation – 'the largest hunt for a serial rapist ever conducted in London'. After 1998 and the second rape, a team of detectives, primarily responsible normally for murder inquiries, had hunted the Stalker. The size of the team varied from time to time, but, in 1999, 2003 and 2009, the area where Grant operated was flooded with police, and at the time of the arrest in 2009 up to 100 officers were involved. He said it was not possible to total the cost but it would run into 'many millions of pounds'.

The judge said to him that he understood that five boroughs had been affected by the crimes. Mr Laidlaw replied, 'That level of fear would have existed in an area of south east London extending into Surrey and Kent,' and the judge said, 'It seems to me that many thousands were living in fear.'

Mr Griffiths, on behalf of Grant, said the offences were 'uniquely revolting' but asked the judge to bear in mind Grant's age.

Then came time for sentence to be passed on the Night Stalker. Grant rose to his feet in the same languid manner he had displayed throughout his trial, as if it was all too boring to be of interest to him. It was of interest to the rest of the world, however, and Judge Peter Rook went straight to the point.

'Your utter depravity knows no bounds,' he told Grant. 'You have been convicted by the jury of 29 offences; most of them are very grave offences. The 18 victims of your offending were all elderly. In respect of nine of them, not only did you break into their homes in the middle of the night, that invasion being a highly traumatic experience for them in itself, but you then proceeded to subject them to humiliating and degrading sexual attacks.

'Your offending spanned a period of 17 years. Five south London boroughs were affected by your offending. Over 17 years, you have terrified a whole community. As your counsel accepted, thousands of people in south London have been living in fear that they might be your next victim. It also led to an enormous drain on police resources as the years went by and you evaded arrest. Your offending led to the largest hunt for a serial rapist ever conducted in London.

'This series of offences have multiple aggravating features. Your offending falls in a category of its own way above anything envisaged in the definitive sentencing guidelines.

'You targeted elderly victims living alone. Your actions blighted the remaining years of their lives. Their homes, where many of them had lived for years, should have been their safest refuge where they could expect to live their lives undisturbed and at peace. You chose to invade their homes when they were in bed at night. It is hard to imagine the extreme fear that feel of your gloved hand and the sight of your masked figure looming over your victims in their beds must have instilled in your defenceless and vulnerable victims.

'Those who you raped or attempted to rape were all over 80. Only one of those you indecently or sexually assaulted was under 80. She was 77. Many of your victims were in poor health. For example, one had severe chronic arthritis in all joints, another had Parkinson's Disease. One had only returned from hospital the day before, one was suffering from Alzheimer's.

'Since, in every case but one, your elderly victims lived on their own, I can only conclude that these offences were well planned and you targeted victims. Singling out your victims must have involved considerable planning as you chose the most vulnerable of people. You would heavily disguise yourself. You covered your face with balaclava or mask. You took tools with you. Often, you removed a whole window pane to gain entry. Once you gained entry through a window which was triple-locked. You removed light bulbs and removed fuses so your offending was committed in darkness with only the light of the torch you carried. You would disconnect the telephone. In the middle of the night, you would wake your victims who would be sleeping in their own beds by placing a gloved hand over their mouths to stop them screaming. You would shine your torch into their terrified eyes. In nine cases, you carried out serious sexual attacks upon your victims. They feared for their lives. You would search their homes and steal their money.

'I have read all the victim impact statements. I have also had the benefit of hearing from one of your victims who courageously gave evidence before me today. I have also heard from the daughter of one of your other victims. You blighted the lives of all your victims. They were all profoundly affected by your actions. Their confidence was irreparably undermined – even those who formerly regarded themselves as strong and independent. Their lives were deeply unsettled. Relations noticed a rapid deterioration in their health.

'Following your offences, some feared to go out. Some never returned to their homes. One movingly said that she no longer loved her home. She felt alone. She could not wait to move. Others suffered continual acute anxiety in fear of possible repetition. They became obsessive about security and feared every unfamiliar noise at night. A son of one of the victims writes, "Since the burglary my mother has become very nervous and withdrawn into herself. It seems to have knocked her confidence completely. I would say that it has ruined the winter years of my mother's life as she has to live with this for the rest of her life."

'In short, your actions lived with them for the rest of their lives. One victim wrote her life was ruined. Mrs J told me today that time has not erased memories. Your victims' lives were changed forever.

'It is also clear from reading the victim impact bundle that has been prepared for me that the impact of your crimes went beyond the impact upon your victims, deeply affecting their families and friends and their daily lives as they cared for your victims. They have suffered mentally. Families have had to change their lives.

'I am not going to catalogue in detail the trail of distress, fear and misery you have left behind you. I will be referring to some of your offences. That should not in any way belittle the impact of your offending has had on *all* your victims.

'Your first offence, rape, count two. At night, having broken into her bungalow, you went into Miss A's bedroom, rushed to her and forced a black gloved hand over her mouth. You held both sides of her face trying to put your tongue into her mouth. Her protests that you were hurting her had no effect upon you. You pulled down her trousers. You raped her whilst she shouted and screamed, telling you to stop. You ejaculated inside her. Since that incident, she could not stay any more at her bungalow.

'Indecent assault and attempted rape, counts four and five. Mrs B was aged 81, not in good health, both hips replaced, severe chronic arthritis in all her joints which made movement very difficult. She walked with a stick with difficulty and was almost housebound. She lived alone in her bungalow in Warlingham since her husband died. She awoke to find you wearing a black mask standing over her. You put your hand over her mouth. You put your fingers in her vagina – it felt unpleasant and sharp – before forcing her legs apart, climbing upon her and trying to penetrate her with your penis. You continued despite all her attempts to persuade you to stop. You tried to pull her legs apart. You ejaculated between her legs. For Mrs B, it was not only terrifying and degrading. It was particularly painful in the light of Mrs B's chronic arthritis.

'You defied detection for many years. From August 1999, you took steps to wash out traces of your DNA and semen.

'Rape, Mrs G, count 13. Mrs G was disturbed when asleep. She got up to investigate and as she went into the living room you grabbed her and placed that gloved hand over her mouth. After stealing her money, you pushed her back on the bed, removed her knickers, pushed her legs open, you inserted first your fingers then your penis into her vagina. It felt horrible. You made her take off her nightie, which you then placed in a washing-up bowl of water to try and wash off your semen. After this, she did not feel safe back at the house, which she had always considered to be secure.

'Rape, count 18, Mrs I. Mrs I suffered from arthritis and a heart condition, aged 88. At 3am, she was awoken by you standing at the foot of her bed. You were wearing a cat-type suit and a balaclava and gloves. You had a torch. You covered her face and mouth with your hand.

'She told you that there was no money in the bedroom, but her purse was in the living room. You pushed her into the living room. Having removed money from her purse, you dragged her across to a settee and positioned her on the edge. You pulled up her nightdress and attempted to rape her. Your penis may have entered her anus – she felt an awful searing pain. Then you raped her, forcing her legs apart and shining a torch into her vaginal area. Mrs I says you were really brutal, ramming your penis in and out of her vagina. She experienced acute searing pain right up inside her.

'You seriously injured Mrs I. She was taken to hospital where she was to undergo surgery for tears to her vagina and damage to her abdominal cavity. It was a life-saving operation. She had to have a colostomy. There was damage to the surface of the rectum. She was in hospital one month, then a nursing home for two months. She had to return to the hospital to have the colostomy reversed. She then moved into a warden-assisted bedsit. As a result of the operations, she had horrific scars on her body. Her doctor states that, although she did make a good recovery, she never really came to terms with the colostomy.

'It was not just serious physical injury that she suffered. She suffered serious psychological impact from your attack. She was never to return home but instead she moved into sheltered accommodation, where she was to stay until she died in 2006. In a witness statement in 2002, she complained about nightmares about the intruder. Her last precious years of life were completely blighted.

'Your depravity included offences against elderly men. Your compulsion to commit these wicked offences was still continuing in the summer of 2009. By this time, you had been supplied with a new Vauxhall Zafira for the benefit of your wife who suffers from multiple sclerosis. You used it to carry on your campaign of offending.

'Just four months before your arrest, Mr O, counts 25 and 26, Thornton Heath. Mr O, aged 88, was disturbed by sounds and went down to investigate. He was confronted by your masked figure. You told Mr O to go back to his bedroom where you told him to undress. Mr O thought that he was about to be murdered, and you would produce a knife. He prayed for a quick death. You then behaved in a depraved way, handling his penis and further demeaning him.

'This offence is an example of two later offences, when you stole credits cards and tried to obtain PIN numbers from your victims. It is clear from the CCTV and clothes found in the Vauxhall when you were arrested you would heavily disguise yourself when trying to extract cash from cash machines.

'You have never shown any remorse. You appear to have no feelings whatsoever for your victims, or indeed your own family or former family. In a desperate attempt to try and escape the consequences of your conduct, you first tried to pass the blame on to one of your sons, and then in this court you sought to blacken the name of your ex-wife accusing her of truly wicked conduct. The jury have rejected your preposterous explanation for the finding of your semen in intimate samples taken from your victims.

'I do not increase your sentence because you pleaded not guilty. However, these accusations are an illustration of your complete amorality. You do have 27 previous convictions. I accept that you have no history of sexual offending, so it appears you began this course of depraved offending when you were in your early thirties. None of your previous offences were anywhere near the level of seriousness of these offences. However, you did receive a prison sentence for robbery when you were 24.

'There can be only one sentence and that is life imprisonment. Discretionary life sentences are reserved for the most serious and grave cases. Some of these offences fall into that category. I have no doubt that these offences are of such seriousness that a life sentence is appropriate to reflect the public abhorrence at your offending.'

The judge continued, 'Rape and attempted rape, count

2, count 5, count 13, count 18 – four concurrent sentences of life imprisonment. In respect of those counts I have to set a minimum sentence. May I make it clear that is the earliest date that you can be considered for release. You will only be released if the parole board considers it is safe to do so. I have no doubt that you are a very dangerous man capable of committing heinous crimes and causing incalculable harm to people. It will be a matter for the parole board whether you are ever released. It may be that you will never be released.

'These offences are far more serious than those envisaged in the Sexual Offences Definitive Guideline, and in the circumstances I must depart from the guideline. They are wholly exceptional. Your offending is in a league of its own. The minimum sentences on the rapes and attempted rape will reflect all your offending in all 29 offences. Here there were nine offences of the utmost gravity: three rapes, one attempted rape, five indecent assaults and one sexual assault.

'I must look at the totality of your offending. I bear in mind that you are now 53. If this was a determinate sentence, a total sentence of 54 years would be appropriate. This means the minimum term will be one of 27 years, less time you have spent in custody. I am told that is one year and 129 days. That makes the total minimum sentence 25 years 236 days. I stress that is the minimum term you must serve.

'It will follow automatically that you will be placed on the Sexual Offenders register for life.'

The minimum sentence imposed would make the convicted Grant nearly 80 by the time it was completed, and even then he might not taste freedom again as it would be a matter for the parole board whether he was ever freed. In the words of the judge, 'It may be that you will never be released.'

At last, the old folk he had rampaged amongst could sleep safely and soundly in their beds again. Delroy Grant was to be locked up in jail until he became an old man – as old as the men and women he had terrified for so many years.

CHAPTER FIFTEEN

Within hours of Delroy Grant's arrest, police realised that he had slipped through their fingers years before – on more than one occasion. A quick check confirmed their worst fears. It revealed that the name Delroy Grant had been mentioned in the hunt for the Stalker and that meant his reign of terror lasted a decade longer than it should have. One officer connected with the case put it succinctly, 'We knew the shit would hit the fan.'

The news of the blunders first emerged publicly in November 2009 when Grant made his first court appearances. By the time Judge Rook jailed him in March 2011, it was featuring prominently in the media coverage of the case and even came to dominate it.

Scotland Yard estimated that 203 victims in total had suffered at his hands, but unofficially the figure was thought to be far higher – perhaps even an incredible thousand or more spread over two decades. The first offence he was charged with took place in 1992, but he had probably started even before then. If, however, he had been caught when his name was first mentioned in 1999, many, if not the majority, of those elderly men and women he offended against would have been spared.

It was in the late 1990s that the link between the crimes against elderly occupants in south London became such that Operation Minstead had been set up. In May 1999, information came in that should have given officers all they needed to close in on the man they wanted. A member of the public who had witnessed a man acting suspiciously near the scene of a burglary in Bromley contacted police with the registration number of the BMW belonging to the suspect. The Driving and Vehicle Licence Authority records showed police that the owner was a Delroy Easton Grant, who lived in Brockley. Officers in Bromley noticed that the burglary had similarities to the Night Stalker crimes and referred it to the Operation Minstead team.

A temporary female detective working in the unit ran the name through the police national computer and found six Delroy Grants, one of whom was already on the national DNA database. Officers focused on that Delroy Grant, who lived in Hackney, east London, almost 20 miles from where the attacks were happening. When police checked his DNA against a sample from one of the crime scenes, it did not match, so the name Delroy Grant was ruled out of the investigation. An officer did go to the 'real' Delroy Grant's address and spoke to his wife who confirmed he still owned the BMW. Grant, however, was out at the time and no one went back to interview him or take a DNA sample.

The other mistake came two years later when the case featured on the BBC's *Crimewatch* programme and a viewer called in to say they thought the Night Stalker was Delroy Grant. When records were checked, it was seen that Delroy Grant had been ruled out earlier, so they did not pursue it.

Also, one woman who had encountered the Stalker when he broke into her home was asked if she knew any black men and mentioned the cab firm where Grant had worked as a minicab driver. This was not pursued, although there was later a suggestion that she simply said the only black men she knew worked at that cab firm.

Other avenues were pursued, which, with the benefit of hindsight, proved fruitless. The DNA suggestion that the Stalker came originally from the Windward Islands of Trinidad, Tobago, St Lucia and St Vincent was off target, as he actually came from Jamaica some distance away.

Among other suggestions that proved groundless were that he might ride a motorbike, have a Brighton connection or be light-skinned.

By 2008, the Night Stalker's crimes were on the increase again – probably because Grant, who collected £184 a week as his wife's carer, had run up debts of thousands of pounds and was in desperate need of money. Sometimes, he carried out two or three burglaries in one evening.

The then recently appointed Metropolitan Police Commissioner, Sir Paul Stephenson, ordered a step-change in the Night Stalker inquiry and Detective Chief Inspector Colin Sutton took over the investigation. Detectives used a high-tech control centre normally used for high-risk terrorist and kidnap operations and analysed a host of burglaries to identify an area of Shirley, south London, as the criminal's most popular hunting ground.

Scores of officers, including surveillance specialists and territorial support group members, were drafted in and a police helicopter was also used to hover at high altitude overhead, using powerful infra-red cameras to see in the dark. With the go-ahead from Commissioner Sir Paul, who was braced for a substantial bill, a trap was set on 28 October 2009, with police centring the operation on an area of about one square mile in Shirley. The Night Stalker struck three times, twice just to the north of the area they were concentrating on and once marginally to the south east, and narrowly escaped capture.

The timing of the offences meant that he must have used a vehicle to travel between the houses he targeted and it was highly likely that he had gone down one road, Orchard Avenue. There was little traffic on the road that night and the Vauxhall Zafira he drove, caught on CCTV, was considered to be his possible vehicle. That, in turn, led to officers being on the lookout for a Zafira on the night he was eventually caught. How much longer police could have gone on with such a massive operation is a matter of debate.

It was the errors committed during the course of the inquiry that led to the remarkable scene of Commander Simon Foy reading a statement, an apology, for television cameras outside Woolwich Crown Court after Grant's conviction.

He said, 'Today has seen Delroy Grant brought to justice for the terrible crimes that he committed. Firstly, though, I take this opportunity to pay tribute to his victims and recognise the traumatic experiences they have been through. They have shown immense courage and dignity throughout the investigation, despite having suffered such terrifying ordeals.

'Part of Grant's method was to prey upon the elderly and take advantage of their frailty and the fact that they would often be too terrified to contact police or indeed even talk about what had happened to them. His victims have worked with us, shared what must have been distressing information with us, and helped us to build up a picture of Grant over many years.

'Grant is a perverted, callous and violent individual. He is a sexual predator, he is a rapist, he is a night-time burglar who preyed on the most vulnerable section of our society. He has said nothing to us about his offending and has not, as far as we know, shown any sign of remorse for what he has done.

'The MPS [Metropolitan Police Service] has never given up in its efforts to try and find Grant. Since 1998, this has been a continuous and long-lasting investigation, undertaken by the specialist crime command. It has, however, been very much a team effort by the MPS and I know from my personal observation and experience that every officer who was involved in the hunt for this man shared an absolute determination to catch him.

'In reacting to what was an escalation of his offending behaviour in the early part of 2009, the Commissioner was very clear in authorising what was a step-change in the level of investigation required – and from which he was ultimately arrested.

'In 1999, there was an opportunity to have identified and apprehended Grant but that opportunity was unfortunately missed. When this came to light, after his arrest, we voluntarily referred the matter to the IPCC [Independent Police Complaints Commission]. The IPCC has completed its report and has recommended that the MPS gives words of advice to officers involved and this has now been done.

'It is appropriate for the MPS to apologise now for this missed opportunity that led to his continued offending for so long afterwards. We are deeply sorry for the harm suffered by all those other victims and for our failure to bring Grant to justice earlier.

'Again, I would like to pay tribute to the courage of Delroy Grant's victims, some of whom I have met this morning and some of whom sadly are not alive today to see him convicted, and to hope that they and their families will feel a sense of relief that he has been caught and brought to justice.'

The IPCC report, published on 24 March, made unpleasant reading for some involved in the case. It said, 'An Independent Police Complaints Commission investigation has found that confusion over a suspect and a poor response to a burglary led to the failure to arrest a serial sex attacker sooner.

'The IPCC began an independent investigation in December 2009 after the Metropolitan Police referred concerns that the man convicted today, Delroy Easton Grant of SE4, should have been arrested earlier for these offences. The offences are also known as the Minstead offences.

'The IPCC investigation found that a crime report from a borough burglary team included information about two different men with similar names, which led to the Operation Minstead team checking the DNA sample of the wrong man against the offender profile. This mistake then contributed to a number of basic investigation enquiries not being done by either team of detectives.

'The IPCC found a case to answer for misconduct for three officers as a result of the investigation. In May 1999 the officers were a Temporary Detective Constable and a Detective Sergeant with Bromley Borough and a Detective Constable with Operation Minstead. Local misconduct meetings have been agreed as appropriate for the officers, two of whom remain with the MPS while the Bromley Detective Sergeant is on secondment from them to another law enforcement organisation.'

The IPCC Commissioner for London, Deborah Glass,

added, 'Delroy Grant's terrible crimes targeted some of society's most vulnerable individuals, leaving them and their loved ones heavily traumatised.

'The IPCC investigated the police's response to one crime linked to Operation Minstead in 1999. It is clear that a simple misunderstanding had horrific consequences. Police missed the opportunity because confusion led to the wrong man's DNA being compared.

'This mistake set off a chain of events that was compounded by poor communications between, and within, the two teams meaning that basic enquiries, such as arresting Grant and searching his property, were not done. Had an officer from either team done this, then Grant may have been charged for the Bromley burglary, leading to his DNA being matched to the Minstead crimes.

'While our investigation identified poor communication and basic policing errors, in which each team believed that the other was responsible, we also have to recognise that we have required officers to account for actions taken 12 years ago, and accept that they could not have foreseen the consequences.'

The IPCC investigation also looked at how the information received was handled, and why it did not lead to Delroy Grant being arrested at the time. The relevant legislation affecting the police actions at the time of the Bromley burglary was also considered. In May 1999, police could only obtain a DNA sample from a person charged with a recordable offence, of which burglary is one. The power to take DNA following arrest for a recordable offence came into effect in April 2004.

'In late May 1999, MPS officers in Bromley responded to a burglary at the home of an elderly woman. Sometime between midnight and 6.25am an air vent was removed and the offender gained entry to the home and stole property. The woman was asleep at the time and was not woken. The offence was reported to police at 6.25am and after an examination of the scene no forensic leads were identified.

'Three days later a member of the public told the police a man had been seen putting on a balaclava and gloves before heading to a house. The registration of the BMW car the man drove was also passed on to officers.

'On receipt of the information, officers from Bromley Borough's burglary team conducted initial checks and identified that the car was registered to Delroy Easton Grant of SE4 and his wife. A search of police databases identified a number of men with a similar name nationwide, including one in London. Delroy Easton Grant was not on the database though.

'Given some of the characteristics of the incident, Bromley Borough's burglary team contacted the Operation Minstead investigation team to inform them of a possible linked crime. The crime report included details of Delroy Easton Grant and the similarly named person in London.

'The crime report resulted in the Operation Minstead team creating a suspect profile, reference N253, using the details of the similarly named man who already had a

DNA profile available to the police. A Detective Constable on Operation Minstead was then tasked to "Trace Implicate Eliminate N253 as Minstead suspect and establish if he is the owner of BMW...".

'A number of entries on the MPS's crime recording system (CRIS) chart the various actions and communications that followed:

'On 29 July a Borough Detective Sergeant (DS) agreed his team would progress enquiries regarding the BMW and its owner.

'On 9 August an Operation Minstead DC updated CRIS to say, "The DNA of suspect re Operation Minstead is not identical with suspect listed in this report."

'On 20 August the Operation Minstead DC noted he had visited the Brockley Mews address and spoken to a woman who "informed me that Mr Grant still owned the vehicle." The DC told the IPCC investigation he had gone to the address as a favour for his borough colleagues.'

The IPCC investigation checked 'electronic footprints' on the CRIS system from when people accessed the report. The Bromley Borough Temporary DC, who made initial contact with the Operation Minstead team and retained lead officer responsibility for borough enquiries, checked the CRIS on 23 July and 25 August but otherwise took no further action. The Bromley Borough DS believed that the Minstead team were carrying out the investigation into the burglary, despite the fact that the Bromley DC was still shown as the officer in the case.

The IPCC investigation found that, irrespective of who

should have conducted further enquiries, there were a number of basic actions that were not undertaken in relation to the Bromley burglary. These included not taking statements from the victim or the witness, obtaining details of the stolen items, and arresting Grant and searching his home for stolen property.

'Given the legislation in place in May 1999, Delroy Easton Grant's DNA would only have been matched to the Minstead series had he been charged with an offence or provided a sample voluntarily. As the enquiries were not conducted, it cannot definitively be said whether enough evidence would have been recovered to charge Grant and obtain his DNA and therefore link him to Minstead offences.'

Despite the points raised in the final paragraph of the IPCC report, the 1999 slip-up attracted widespread criticism.

DCI Sutton, who had retired from the force by the time Grant's trial began, said, 'There is evidence he could have been committing crimes all the way back to 1987. It is quite reasonable to think he committed over 1,000 break-ins, of which a substantial number would have involved sexual assaults.

'I was very proud of the team that we caught him after 17 days but unfortunately we'd been trying for 17 years.'

In one interview, Mr Sutton admitted frankly, 'I was really quite appalled. There was a very small band of dedicated and very loyal officers but they were following a thankless task of trying to get DNA from so many people in south east London. It was a very, very slow process and it was not really how they thought the case could be solved and certainly it proved that. It had been an unsuccessful investigation for many years.

'I think the leadership was blinkered almost down the DNA route and did not take other opportunities which could have been successful. If you add on to that the individual errors – and individual errors can happen in any investigation, people are human, police officers doing investigations are human.

'But the 1999 error meant that Delroy Grant, just the name Delroy Grant, was in the database as eliminated for ever more.

'The lines of enquiry were almost trying to be too clever – trying to do things like looking at the ancestral element of the DNA profile or looking to see if the DNA could give us an indication of the man's physical appearance. That's cutting-edge science that's really, really difficult to do, when in fact what was needed was not for us to behave as a clever, sophisticated murder squad, but for us to behave as a burglary squad – because we were trying to catch a burglar and we needed to behave like a burglary squad. And in fact that is what happened in the end.'

Mr Sutton, no longer a serving officer, actually posted a lengthy blog that day, 24 March, about the case It included the comment: 'Once more we have a Met Commander apologising live on all news channels, repeated in case you missed it at 6, 6.30 and 10. At least

Simon Foy ventured away from the revolving sign and down to Woolwich to meet real people, real victims, and say sorry in person. But I imagine I am not alone in asking, in these circumstances, "What for? What went wrong? Who messed up?"'

He added, 'In May 2009 when I first went across to Lewisham to "have a look, see if there is a way of solving it" (as was my brief) it was pretty obvious that we never would. As I later learned from the decision logs, virtually everything for the past 11 years had been based on DNA. Even when on occasion some creativity or lateral thinking was employed, it was getting scientists to try to discern ancestry or physical characteristics from the DNA profile. It was all about the DNA.'

Mr Sutton also referred to the 'hopeless' task of getting DNA from a list of more than 20,000 men. 'The second thing which appalled me in May 2009 was the size of the team. Or, more precisely, the lack of size of the team. Minstead had been culled in 2004 when officers had to be plundered from HSCC to bolster Safer Neighbourhood Teams. Having already cut three murder teams, when Sir Ian [Blair, Met. Commissioner from 2005 to 2008] came calling again, Minstead felt the knife and was halved in size. Effectively in May 2009 there were eight people trying to get all these DNA swabs. In my first week they returned with one solitary swab. As we then had 5,200 men on the priority list the arithmetic was striking – at that rate it was 100 years of work.'

Mr Sutton continued, '... once we were looking for the

Night Stalker on the streets at night and not in a database during the day time, we got him. The tragedy is that it took so long.'

Warming to his theme, Mr Sutton asked, 'Where do we go from here? What is important is that this is all never to happen again. For me, top of the list is that those who are the decision-makers in major investigations realise that an unknown DNA profile is conclusive evidence of presence, and so often of guilt, but that it is a very blunt, unsophisticated and ultimately unsuccessful means of identifying a suspect from a large population. Mass screenings seldom work, often deflect focus and always cost the earth.'

Returning to the case a week later, he blogged again, saying that he felt a 'new and independent inquiry' should be launched into the lengthy Operation Minstead investigation.

Mr Sutton was one of the few to have had a conversation with Grant when the Stalker was in custody in Lewisham police station and he remarked on it. 'He seemed totally unconcerned. I had a conversation with him about cricket. It was a blokey, friendly conversation like you'd have in a bar. In a strange way he was quite a nice chap and that was what everybody we spoke to said. "It can't be Delroy..." But he had this other side to his character which he hid very well.'

One man who was keener than most to see the Night Stalker brought to justice was Det. Supt. Simon Morgan, who had been appointed Senior Investigating Officer of

Operation Minstead in 2001. He sat in court every day of the trial.

After the jury had reached its verdict, he spoke of the difficulties his men had faced, both professionally and personally. 'For someone to prey on the elderly and for them not to have peace and comfort in the latter years of their life was just horrendous. If I put you in the position of a victim – you are in your eighties and you are in your bed, you are safe, and you are woken in the middle of the night by a hand over your mouth and immediately there will be a demand for sex. You reach for the light to turn it on and nothing happens because he has already disabled the electrics. He shines a torch in your eyes and he is wearing a balaclava. You are petrified – and I'm going to ask you now to describe him to me. It is impossible – you just can't.'

Mr Morgan also talked on *Crimewatch*, the programme that had tried several times to help catch the Night Stalker, about the near-miss when Grant had struck just outside the area being monitored by police. He said the team were 'absolutely devastated. We had invested an immense amount of proactive resources into covering a favoured area and he switches to an area that he had never been at before.'

The detective also talked of the reasons he thought Grant became especially active – 'The motivation appeared to be mainly for money. It was clear that the level of precautions that he had been taking in the planning of the offences was reducing. He was becoming greedy' – and of the night that he was finally caught.

'I received a phone call at 2am to tell me that we had finally apprehended the man that I personally had been waiting eight years to meet. He matched very accurately what we thought we knew about him. He is a primary carer for his disabled wife who has multiple sclerosis. He has a history of working in old people's homes. We knew that he was out working the night often as a minicab driver. His family and friends that we have spoken to are absolutely shocked that this is him. He was outwardly Mr Ordinary. He clearly lived two lives and he kept his two lives separate. Nobody knew he was the man that was out raping the elderly.

'I went straight into work and went down to the custody suite to meet him. Clearly, I have waited a long time for this moment. I also wanted to know what was the reason why he had taken such precaution to hide his face from the victims. He has no front teeth and does not wear dentures and that would have been something that if a victim had noted we would have probably and highly likely caught him a lot earlier. He was a one in a billion [DNA] match – it was him.'

Mr Morgan said that Grant's accusation that his wife planted his DNA was a 'ludicrous' defence. 'If it was not so sad, it would be laughable. Personally, I waited ten years for this verdict. For years, many of his victims, all they wanted to know was who was he and why did he attack them. Sadly, many of them have gone to the grave not knowing the answers to those questions. His victims have shown courage and strength when faced with the most frightening of situations. These are traits that Delroy Grant does not possess. He is now rightly where he belongs.'

Grant had hidden that dark side of his character all those years before from his young bride Janet. She soon realised the type of man she had married and they had, as we have heard, divorced only for him to reappear in her life years later with his amazing story of her obtaining, storing and then planting his semen and saliva in order that his DNA would incriminate him.

Her reaction to his attempt to avoid retribution for his crimes was succinct: 'I hope he suffers every day in prison,' she said. 'He is an evil man. I was never going to let him win. There must be something very wrong with him to think he'd get away with saying I did all that just to spite him.'

Of his defence that she had hoarded his bodily fluids to plant them at a dozen crime scenes, she said, 'I could see people laughing in the public gallery. When I left court, I thought, "He's going to get what he deserves."'

At the time of Grant's arrest in November 2009, Janet had hinted at his true character. But after his conviction she was able to talk in more detail of the 'misery' he had put her through. 'Being with him was a living hell. He would attack me in front of my children, beat me while I was pregnant and cheat on me with other women. Anything could start it off. If I hadn't cleaned the house properly – if there was a speck of dust under the bed – he would scream in my face: "You're gonna get a beating!"

'When I was pregnant with my second son Michael, he attacked me so badly I thought I would lose my baby. He punched me to the ground, then kicked me in the stomach. He even hit me when I'd just gone into labour.'

She added, 'Michael had to have an operation a month after he was born because of the trauma Delroy had caused him. His stomach had become tangled inside his tiny body because the beatings were so ferocious. At one stage, I didn't know if he'd survive.'

Although she added she reported his behaviour to the police, she said, 'At the time no one took domestic violence seriously, let alone the police. I knew Delroy was dangerous, because he was so scheming. He could be charm itself and turn into a monster in a second.'

His stepdaughter Shirley, by this time in her thirties, said, 'I remember Dad taking me to see another woman he said was my auntie. Later, I told Mum and she asked me to show her the house. He'd been playing away again. When we went round, Delroy was there.'

Another of the women in his life at the time he was carrying out the Night Stalker raids said, 'He had extreme mood swings and was very controlling. He would really scare me. He would lose his temper and just lash out at me. Anything could set him off. He was so possessive. I don't think he trusted women at all.'

The woman, who did not want to be identified, added, 'I liked and loved the person I first met. But then it was like I was bullied and intimidated and made to feel worthless. I was in love with him, but I didn't realise he was gradually taking control of my life. It was as if I was his property.'

The woman, in her fifties at the end of the trial, had had an affair with Grant over a number of years and said she had often thought of ending their relationship, only for him to talk her round. 'I went on with it even though I knew deep down it wasn't right. After his rages, he would say he was sorry and go back to being that nice person again. He was like a Dr Jekyll and Mr Hyde.'

Grant had stopped celebrating Christmas after becoming a Jehovah's Witness and the woman said, 'He believed in demons and was always quoting the Bible, saying he was going to be reborn and live the perfect life. He thought demons could possess you and he once thought there were demons in my house. He didn't like having horror books in the house and would make sure they were thrown out. He actually thought he had seen demons working their evil in front of his eyes.

'At first, he was the perfect gentleman. He was really smartly dressed and could charm anybody who met him for the first time. Once he saw a woman begging outside a shop and gave her £10 he had and told her to do what she liked with it.

'He was very romantic at the start. We went on trips to Brighton as he liked to walk on the beach. He was a good cook and liked taking me to restaurants and getting me to try Jamaican food.'

The woman also said that he did not show any of the perverted sexual side of his life to her. 'There was nothing untoward about our sex life. He was very much a gentleman, very caring and gentle.'

The woman, like everyone who knew Grant, had no clue that he was the monster terrorising a city, although looking back she later realised there might have been telltale clues to his nocturnal prowling. 'He always had cuts on his legs, but he used to claim he got them climbing over fences while playing with his youngest lad Louis or other innocent things like that. There were also times when he would really lay into me for no reason and I wonder now if he had been out doing something the night before. I also wonder if some of his caring side was out of guilt – as if he was trying to make up for his crimes.'

She added that Grant believed the police were everywhere, watching him. 'I thought he was just being paranoid. He would see two people sat in a car and he would say they were spying on him. He could be a bit of a bad boy at times – smoking weed and things like that – but I never dreamt he was capable of being involved in anything really serious.'

Grant's absurd defence, that his ex-wife Janet planted his DNA, may have been inspired by the crime shows he loved to watch on television. 'He was addicted to crime shows on satellite channels,' she said. 'He would spend hours watching them. He wasn't interested in CSI-style dramas or anything fictional – only true crime documentaries. He was totally obsessed with programmes about cold case research and breakthroughs in forensic DNA.'

The woman added, in her interview with the *Daily Mirror*, 'He told me he was brought up by the old lady until he was about 12, but he never mentioned any kind of abuse. He lived in a rural area and would reminisce about going swimming in the river and outdoor things like that. He talked about walking 10 miles to school, feeding the goats and working on his brother's fruit farm. His told me his granny was very strict and came from quite a religious background. His childhood seemed very important to him, but he only ever spoke about the nice things.'

In fact, the woman still had some good memories of Grant, of his being kind and generous to complete strangers. 'I remember he once stopped his car to help a disabled old lady across the road – and he would also give a lift to people if he saw them struggling with heavy bags.'

Kind words about Delroy Grant were hard to find as he began his prison sentence – hardly surprising given the other side of his personality over the years. One man recalled that, when he was a 13-year-old boy, he saw Grant attack his sister, who was going out with Grant at that time.

'What happened that day will stay with me forever. It scarred my sister and it has scarred me too. Grant showed no mercy as she cried out for help. He just left her for dead after he'd finished. He would explode and slap her around. One night he grabbed her by the hair and dragged her into the bedroom. He was shouting, "Why haven't you washed up?" I began to hear screaming and I forced my way in. But he slammed me against the wall so hard I slumped to the floor, nearly unconscious. Then he raped my sister in front of me, just yards away. It was like watching a horror film unfold. He just left her, bloodied and broken, on the bed in front of me. It haunts me every day. Grant should count himself lucky that I wasn't the man who found and arrested him. I'd have killed him.'

Grant's son, Delroy Junior, also spelled out his feelings for the Night Stalker – and his contempt for the way his father had tried to implicate him in the crimes by suggesting police take his son's DNA and compare it with that left at the crimes.

The 35-year-old told of his reaction to hearing that his father had been arrested by the Operation Minstead team. 'I was in shock. I couldn't get my head around the fact my own dad was the man I had heard about on TV. I felt so ashamed. For the next year and a half until his trial, I just lived in a dream world, wondering if I was going to be like my dad. I hated him for what he had done to all those poor old people.'

Then he heard about his father trying to frame him for the crimes. 'My dad has been a let-down all my life. What kind of father tries to frame his own son for the awful, disgusting things he has done to old people? He's not a dad to me – he's nothing but a dog.'

Grant had disappeared from his son's life when he was just a toddler, but he reappeared one day outside the school gates and promised to take both his sons swimming the next day. Delroy Junior said, 'I was so excited to meet my dad, despite everything my mum had said about him. To this day I can still feel the disappointment when he didn't turn up to take us swimming. I was gutted.'

Years later, Delroy Junior and his brother Michael tracked their father down and found him washing his car near his address. 'When I saw him again I didn't know whether I wanted to punch him or hug him. He said he was so sorry for being a bad father. He wasn't sorry at all but he made me believe it at the time. He didn't mention anything about his life. ... I had no idea of the horrendous things he was doing in his spare time. All we knew was that he cared for his wife. But when we left it actually felt good that I had met my real dad again.'

Delroy Junior got to know his father's other sons, although whenever he would go out with his father, the older man never had enough money to pay for his part of the bill – leaving his eldest son to pick up the tab. He also always refused to venture to Delroy Junior's home as he did not want to meet ex-wife Janet.

After the criminal double-life of his father became known, young Delroy even considered changing his own name. 'My name is part of who I am but I hate him so much that I want no one to think that I'm the same as him. To be turned against by your dad is the worst thing in the world. I started to cry when I learned he was trying to frame me and it made me wonder if he ever cared for me at all.'

A fascinating insight into the mind of Delroy Grant – what made him tick and why he did the things he did –

came from psychologist David Holmes. 'In terms of his own self-esteem, he does not want to see himself as what he actually is, because he is a little bit frightened of what he is,' he told the *Daily Telegraph*. 'This means that he is something of a coward. He won't confront. If someone fights back, he is going to run away which seems to fit the pattern here. He will pick on very weak victims.

'I think he sees these people as easy to control, easy people to push around and not leave forensic clues. ... He is somebody who is very controlling. As a result he sees the elderly as being easy targets to control, and he is very meticulous and rigid in the way he goes about things. He uses exactly the same methods each time and this has made it much more easy for police to piece together that the various incidents have been carried out by the same person.

The psychologist added, 'Wearing two sets of clothes and various other small indicators would say that this person is somebody who can be plausible, wants to be plausible, wants to be accepted by these elderly individuals – in fact he is almost doing them a favour. But he is gratifying some basic instinct which is not entirely of the norm, which he is also ashamed of.'

Perhaps the final word should rest with his father George, the devout Christian who came to London on a £65 boat fare in 1961, hoping that his son would one day follow him. He did, only to achieve notoriety 40 years later.

George, by his own admission, had limited contact with Delroy once the boy had grown up. Sometimes, he only heard about the new women in his life through friends. He went to one of his son's weddings, but not the second one to Jennifer, and his son rarely brought his children round to meet their grandfather. It was only later that he heard that Delroy was violent to first wife Janet. 'No one in my family had ever done that,' he said, shaking his head as he sat in an armchair of his neat home in south London.

George never visited his son in jail after he was imprisoned for his part in the post office robbery. 'I was ashamed,' he said, adding, 'The only thing I have ever done wrong is jump a set of traffic lights – and I paid the fine for that.' His son had said that he fell in with the wrong crowd and that led to his early brushes with the law, but his father's response was: 'If you are a good person, company should not lead you astray.

'If he is a man, he has to stand on his own two feet. He has spread his bed hard. I am so sorry for all those people he has done this to.'

When detectives first came to tell Mr Grant of his son's arrest, they were met by his wife Ruby, whose death he feels was hastened by the revelations about Delroy. He was in the house and he heard her say, 'No, not Delroy.' He added, 'What they told me shocked me. I could not believe it.'

Speaking after the sentencing, he said, 'I can't remember when I last saw him, but, if I did, I'd ask him why he did these things. He should get on his knees and ask for a pardon. I can't help him. I did not make him do it. My son is devious. Where he gets it from I don't know. Some people are bad and don't commit themselves to the Lord. Let him get on his knees and let him come to his senses.'

George, who keeps a Bible by his bedside, added, 'I feel such shame. I ask the Lord to see me through. I believe in Heaven and Hell and he will go to Hell if he does not repent.

'The Devil is strong – Delroy must have let the Devil overcome him.'